LANDCRABS AND 3-LITRES

BMC 1800, 2200 (ADO17) AND 3-LITRE (ADO61) CARS

JAMES TAYLOR

AMBERLEY

First published 2025

Amberley Publishing
The Hill, Stroud,
Gloucestershire, GL5 4EP

www.amberley-books.com

ISBN: 978 1 3981 2159 1 (print)
ISBN: 978 1 3981 2160 7 (ebook)

British Library Cataloguing in Publication Data.
A catalogue record for this book is available from the British Library.

Typeset in 10pt on 13pt Celeste.
Typesetting by SJmagic DESIGN SERVICES, India.
Printed in the UK.

Contents

1

In the Beginning

After the Austin and Morris groups had merged in 1952 to form BMC (the British Motor Corporation), it took a while before any real rationalisation of the product range was possible. But by 1955, BMC's Chairman, Sir Leonard Lord, had formulated a plan to sweep away the multitude of models that the corporation had inherited and replace them with a range of just three basic types. To keep the dealer chains happy, these might be made with any combination of the marque badges available to the corporation, but in simple terms he wanted a large saloon, a medium-sized saloon, and a small saloon.

Lord wanted a talented engineer to lead the design teams that would be assigned to these new projects, and he could not find the man he wanted within the pool of engineers already available to him. Mindful of the clever thinking behind the strong-selling Morris Minor of 1948, he sought out the man who had designed it. Alec Issigonis had left Morris in 1952, sensing that trouble might follow the company's merger with Austin, and had

Alec Issigonis was the single-minded designer behind the ADO17, the last in a related three-car range for BMC.

The success of the first of those three cars, the Mini, made Issigonis' reputation. This is the first production example. (BMW)

gone to Alvis. Here, he had designed an advanced new saloon car with an all-aluminium V8 engine, but sadly Alvis could not afford to put it into production and Issigonis realised that he needed a more secure position elsewhere. Lord's approach was timely; Issigonis agreed to rejoin BMC, and was set to work on new designs.

Issigonis arrived back at BMC in 1956 and started work on the large and medium saloons, which were to have engine sizes of around 1500cc and 1200cc respectively. His first design was for the larger model, and despite its rear-wheel-drive configuration, it incorporated a number of the new ideas for which the designer would later become known. A prototype with the engineering project code of XC9000 was built in 1957, but work on it was cut short when Lord instructed him to put all his efforts into designing the new small car – which would be launched in 1959 as the Mini. By the time Issigonis was able to return to XC9000 in 1958, he was convinced that the front-wheel-drive system he had developed for the Mini would be ideal for the larger saloon as well.

An Increase in Size

In the minds of BMC top management, the new cars envisaged in the late 1960s were numbered ADO15 (which became the Mini), ADO16 (which became the 1100), and ADO 17 (the new large car). However, Issigonis continued to use his own system of engineering project codes, and in this scheme the large car in its front-wheel-drive form was XC9001. At least thoughts were aligned on what the new large car was supposed to do: in the medium term, it would replace the 1.5-litre Farina-styled saloons that had been approved for 1959 introduction.

Meanwhile, BMC engineers were working on a new version of the B-series engine for the forthcoming new MG sports model, the MGB. The car had become heavier than originally anticipated, and the 1622cc engine of the MGA in the original plan was not going to give the required performance. An enlargement to 1798cc was under development, and Issigonis thought that the opportunity to put this more powerful engine into his new large saloon – obviously, in transverse form – was too good to miss. To an engineer, it made perfect sense. Unfortunately, he failed to appreciate that the British public perceived a world of difference between a 1.5-litre saloon and a 1.8-litre saloon and that in those days, 1.5-litre saloons sold about four times as well as 1.8-litre saloons.

By this time, Sir Leonard Lord had handed over much of the responsibility for running BMC to his protégé George Harriman, and Harriman was content to trust Issigonis' judgement. The decision to use the 1.8-litre engine therefore seems never to have been questioned – but it would have major implications for the ADO17 project and, ultimately, for the success of the car after it entered production. That bigger engine would be capable of powering a bigger car than had originally been envisaged, and as a result Issigonis lengthened the wheelbase of his proposed saloon by 6 inches compared with the Farina 1.5-litre cars, and widened the car as well. The positive result was an extremely spacious passenger compartment, which would always be one of ADO17's great strengths.

BMC's mid-range cars in the early 1960s were the Farinas, initially released with 1.5-litre engines but by then with 1622cc types. (Alf van Beem. CC0 1.0 Universal Public Domain)

Looks Matter

Issigonis' first prototype of XC9001 looked uncomfortably (but unsurprisingly) like an enlarged Mini, and BMC top management called for some alternative ideas. The BMC team had their proposal ready by October 1958, the first mock-up to reflect the increased size that Issigonis now wanted – and it looked remarkably like the car that would eventually enter production except for a fashionable twin-headlamp front end. Perhaps most notably, it had a six-light design that was associated more with cars in the class above rather than the four-light type favoured in the medium-sized saloons of the day.

Pinin Farina (the name became Pininfarina as one word in 1961) were asked for their ideas, too, and clearly thought that a BMC family resemblance would be welcomed in the way it had been when they had drawn up the 1.5-litre and the larger six-cylinder saloons. Their 1959 proposal therefore looked like an enlarged ADO16 (the 1100, or XC9002 to Issigonis). BMC top management did not like that either, and as a result adopted a compromise solution in which Pininfarina were invited to improve the in-house design.

The Pinin Farina company was asked for thoughts on the new 1.5 litre car early on. This was their 1959 proposal for XC9001.

By March 1962, the car had grown to a 1.8-litre type and the project was known to Issigonis as XC9005. This was a Pininfarina (by now one word) refinement of the BMC design.

Issigonis' designation for the project now changed to XC9005, which appears to mark the transition between a 1.5-litre car and the 1.8-litre size. Pininfarina's revisions to the in-house body design were seen on a mock-up presented in June 1960, and the Italian design house made further minor changes until by March 1962 a satisfactory design was signed off – although even then the proposed grille was changed before production. Most of the Pininfarina revisions had been to the front and rear ends, and the distinctive 'cow's hip' rear-wing styling was one of their suggestions. The centre section of the body that had been drawn up in 1958 remained largely unchanged, although there had been changes to the side window frames.

The Engineering

By this time, Issigonis was using a 'cell' system for engineering development, in which separate teams or cells worked on separate projects. ADO17 was entrusted to B Cell at Longbridge, under the direction of Chris Kingham, but inevitably Issigonis himself kept a close eye on what was happening. In the meantime, the 1.8-litre engine had also been further redesigned, when the single-carburettor engine proved too unrefined for saloon use. Before it reached production, it would gain a five-bearing crankshaft that gave smoother running.

Fundamental to Issigonis' design for ADO17 was the front-wheel-drive layout with a transverse engine that he had pioneered on the Mini. However, there were also many differences between the ADO17 layout and that of the smaller car. There was more room to reinforce the bodyshell in ADO17 than in the Mini, and this enabled Issigonis to dispense with the sub-frames that had been added during Mini development to maintain torsional rigidity. He reinforced the front end by welding a tubular cross-member to the dash, and

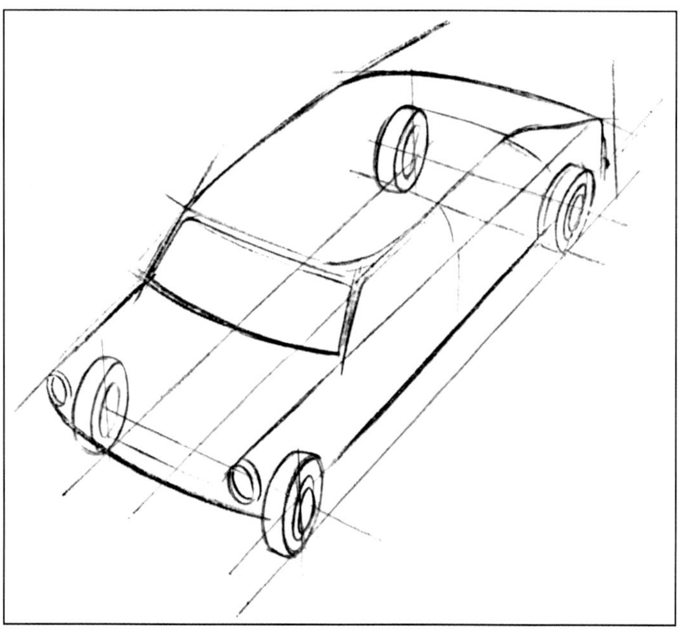

To get the best possible ride and make the best use of space, Issigonis pushed the wheels out to the four corners of the car. This sketch is from one of his notebooks.

The overall layout of the 1800 was proudly illustrated in early sales brochures. The engine was mounted transversely to reduce its length, and the gearbox was mounted below it. Clear in this picture are the spheres of the Hydrolastic suspension.

Above left: This picture was issued by Dunlop, who manufactured elements of the Hydrolastic system. It shows the front suspension.

Above right: The gearchange was mounted conventionally between the front seats, but it acted on the front-mounted gearbox through a system of cables.

was then able to mount the suspension and the engine directly to the bodyshell, with the front Hydrolastic displacers in that tube.

Issigonis had for some time been convinced of the benefits of the Hydrolastic hydraulic suspension system developed by Dr Alex Moulton, and chose this for the ADO17 – although it actually appeared first on the ADO16 1100 models in 1962. The brand name of Hydrolastic combined the words 'hydraulic' and 'elastic', aiming to show that it depended on hydraulic fluid and was very flexible. Instead of road springs it used rubber cones. Underneath them were chambers that contained the hydraulic fluid, which was a mixture of water and anti-freeze and was kept under high pressure within a sealed system. When the front wheels hit a bump, the fluid was forced through spring-loaded conical flap valves that acted as dampers, and deflected the rubber springs. Small-bore pipes connected the front and rear suspension units on each side of the car. Fluid forced out of the front chambers by the front wheels hitting a bump travelled through these pipes to the rear units, so forcing the rear wheels downwards to maintain the car on an even keel.

As for steering, Issigonis knew that he wanted a rack-and-pinion system if only because it was more compact than other systems then in use. For the brakes, he chose discs at the front and drums at the rear, with a valve in the hydraulic line that transferred braking force between front and rear axles when it sensed deceleration. Allied to this was a night dimming system for the lights at the rear of the car: when the sidelights were switched on, a resistor (the 'blue box dimmer') reduced the intensity of the tail, brake and rear indicator lights to prevent them from dazzling following drivers.

Issigonis (left) and Charles Griffin, BMC's Chief Engineer, pose proudly with an early Austin 1800.

Prototype cars came together in 1963, and Issigonis was so confident of the correctness of his design that he called for only three development cars. Not one was tested on the European continent before the launch, apparently because Issigonis was opposed to spending the money on a large number of prototypes and an expensive test programme. It was a decision that BMC would come to regret.

Interior Design

Issigonis' ideas were allowed to prevail in the design of the ADO17 interior, too. There was never any doubt that the sheer size of the passenger compartment would be a strong selling point, but Issigonis famously disliked ornamentation, and he ensured that the interior design was simply functional. The two front seats met in the middle so that they could be set together and used as a bench seat if required, so making the car a full six-seater. There was no rake or backrest adjustment, though, as Issigonis regarded these features as unnecessary.

The steering position has since often been described as bus-like, and scant regard seemed to have been paid to the positioning of the toggle switches on the dashboard. Like the chrome 'umbrella handle' handbrake under the front parcel shelf, some of these proved hard to reach for a driver wearing a seatbelt – which of course had not been a consideration during the design phase when seatbelts were not a regular feature of cars. The strip speedometer was the only concession to modern practice, and the minimalism of that design was arguably what recommended it to Issigonis.

Forecasts

Buoyed up by the success of the ADO15 Mini and by the enthusiastic acceptance of its ADO16 1100 follow-up, BMC management allowed itself to indulge in some optimistic sales forecasts for ADO17. Managing Director George Harriman set a production level of 4,000 cars a week at Longbridge, which implied 200,000 cars a year. Such figures were quite fantastical, and would never even be approached in reality.

At least there seemed to be some recognition that this new 1.8-litre car was not going to be a direct replacement for the Farina saloons of the 1.6-litre A60 family (which was an evolution of 1959's 1.5-litre A55). When the new ADO17 was launched to the press in summer 1964, it was described as an additional model in the BMC range and not as a replacement for the older models. In practice, they would stay in production for another five years to meet demand, as it became clearer and clearer that the 1.8-litre ADO17 was not what buyers in that class wanted – not least because it was around 14 per cent more expensive than the Austin A60 Cambridge.

Finally, and as had probably been understood from the beginning of the ADO17 project, the ADO17 would be released in versions for Austin dealers and versions for Morris dealers that had minor cosmetic differences. Both, though, would be known simply as 1800 models. A photograph of a styling model supposedly dating from November 1962 suggests that BMC were also thinking at this early stage of a Riley derivative, too. This never came to fruition, but the model certainly seems to have influenced the eventual styling of the ADO61 3-litre model (see Chapter 6).

2

The Mk I Models, 1964–68

When the ADO16 1100 range had been introduced in 1962, Morris dealers had received their cars a year before Austin dealers. This was probably because space became available to install the new production lines at the Morris factory in Cowley before it became available at Austin's Longbridge factory. However, to redress the balance, the new 1800 was introduced as an Austin first and as a Morris nearly two years later. Denying the new model to half of its dealer outlets for so long can have done nothing to improve its sales in the early days.

The press launch for the Austin 1800 was held in Scotland during July and August 1964, and was based at the Strathgarve Lodge Hotel in Garve, Ross and Cromarty. Showroom availability began on 13 October, and the new car made its formal public appearance at the London Motor Show that opened on 21 October. As usual, the Austin Motor Company had a large stand and displayed the full range of its models, and alongside the Minis, 1100s, A60s, A40s and A110 Westminsters was a single 1800.

Austin offered two models. The standard 1800 had neither heater-demister nor bumper over-riders, both of which were extra-cost options. The De Luxe model came with both as standard, plus dual windtone horns, a passenger sun visor, leather upholstery, rear door armrests, moulded carpets, opening quarter-lights, sill tread plates, cantrail grab handles, and wheel discs. For those who really wanted to push the boat out, there were also two options for the De Luxe model in the shape of reclining front seats and a centre rear armrest (although in practice these were not available until December 1964). At £808 14*s* 7*d*, which included £140 14*s* 7*d* Purchase Tax, the new 1800 De Luxe was the second most expensive model in the Austin line-up, behind the A110 Westminster.

When the respected weekly *Autocar* magazine tested an early 1800 for its issue of 23 October 1964, its testers were very impressed. 'There are so many good points in the design of this latest BMC product that it is difficult to single out the best,' they wrote. 'The new Austin 1800 ... is undoubtedly one of the most important cars in the world of motoring'.

They thought that 'the whole car feels and looks robust' and that it had 'exceptional roadholding powers' while the ride was 'very good indeed, over any road surface including *pavé*, with almost complete absence of sideways roll'. The 1.8-litre engine was 'sweet and quiet on the whole, but there was some gear clatter and tinkling when it was idling'.

Above: The cover of this early sales brochure shows an interesting focus on design details: the buying public was clearly expected to have heard of both Issigonis and Pininfarina.

Below: This early press picture shows one of the first cars, badged as an Austin 1800 but built at the Morris plant in Cowley and registered with the Oxford licensing authorities.

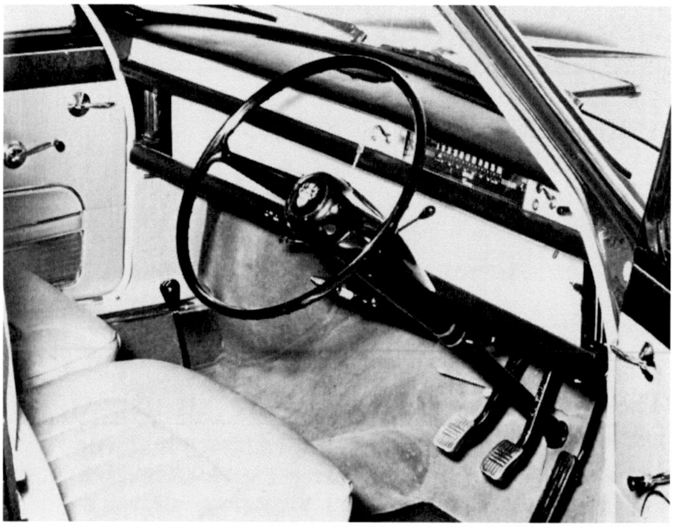

The dashboard was very plain, with a strip speedometer that was a concession to contemporary fashion. The steering wheel was set at an angle that reminded some commentators of driving a bus.

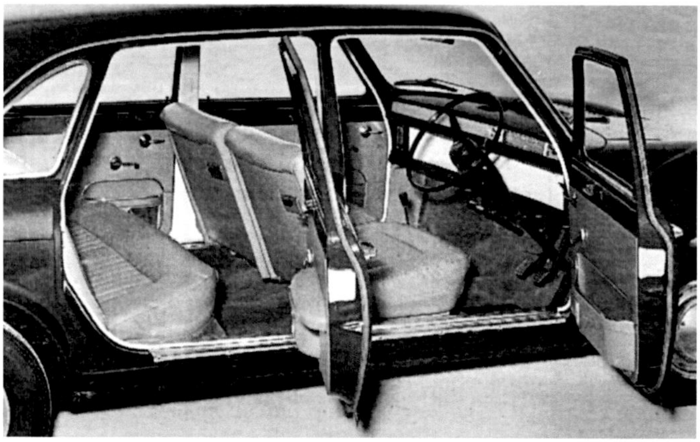

The outstanding feature of the ADO17 was always its interior space. Few cars in the luxury class could match it, and none in the 1.8-litre class came close.

The biggest disappointment was the steering, which required 'excessive arm movements' and would also have been much better with a smaller steering wheel and a more steeply raked column. On one occasion during the test, 'sudden avoiding action was needed, and in these circumstances the steering did prove to be disconcertingly slow'. There was some drumming (which was related to engine speed rather than road speed), the handbrake was not powerful enough, and the fuel consumption was 'not as good as we had hoped for'. Overall, though, *Autocar* certainly liked the car, and suggested that after the Mini and the 1100 this new model might just have achieved a hat-trick of successes for Issigonis and BMC.

The First Two Years

In January 1965, BMC announced they were freeing up extra production capacity for the 1800 by transferring assembly of A60 models to Cowley. That same month, the first production changes were made in response to early customer feedback. The markings on the original dipstick were not legible if the stick was inserted back to front, and this had caused some owners to overfill the engine with oil, so a revised dipstick was introduced. Valve noise at high speeds was cured by reducing the valve clearances, which also had the effect of reducing top-end power by 2bhp. In addition, the 4.19:1 final drive ratio of the early cars was changed to the 3.88:1 ratio used on the prototypes. Bizarrely, BMC described this as a response to oil consumption problems.

More considered changes were introduced for the 1966 models that went on sale in October 1965. The handbrake was repositioned at a different angle, and the rear anti-roll bar was deleted. Then at the end of the year there were some changes to the rear suspension, and the steering was adjusted to cure tyre scuffing. January 1966 brought improved engine mounting rubbers that did not part company with the metal plates to which they were bonded, and stronger engine side covers. Then in February came a gearbox modification to prevent the lever jumping out of first and second, a spacer to cure steering rattle, and shields to prevent water affecting the rear hubs.

BMC placed this advertisement in the catalogue for the 1964 Earls Court Motor Show. The emphasis on the 'revolutionary' aspects of the design was spot-on; the question of elegance was more a matter of opinion.

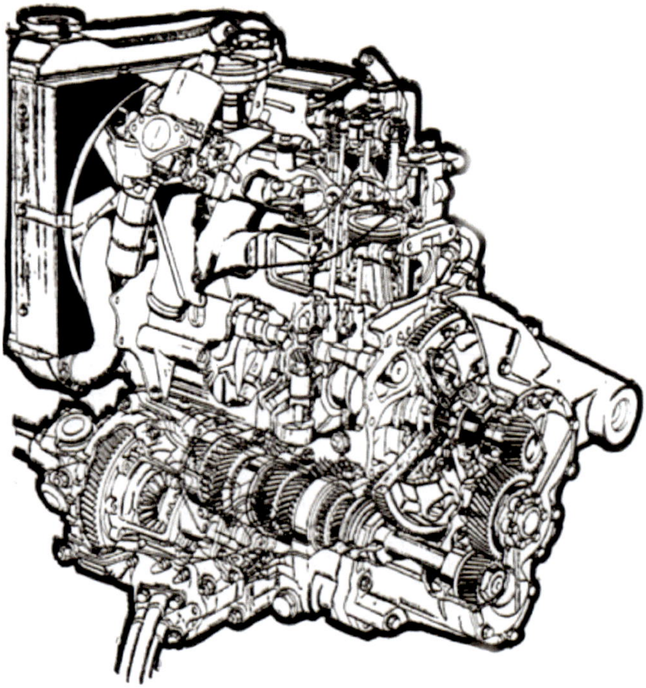

Left: The 1.8-litre engine was a transverse version of the B-series designed for north–south use in the MGB sports car, although the saloon had only one carburettor instead of two. This cutaway drawing, showing the engine as it would have been seen from the back, shows how the radiator was mounted at the side of the engine bay.

Below: This 1967 Austin 1800 displays a colour characteristic of BMC products at the time. (Steve Knight/Flickr)

The characteristic 'cow's hips' of the 1800 are seen on this Austin variant pictured in Spain. The Mk I had these horizontal light units. (Spanish Coches, CC by 2.0)

These improvements were welcome, but they did nothing to address the undeniable fact that the 1800 was not selling well. Even winning the European Car of the Year award in 1965 did not make a lasting difference, and the ADO17 sales figures must have been a huge disappointment to BMC. Against George Harriman's projected 200,000 cars a year, the Austin version of the car had managed a miserable 25,395 in its first year on sale. The 1966 season was much better, but the total of 56,876 built in that year would actually be the best the ADO17 ever achieved. Still, there was room for optimism at this stage: the Morris version of the car had not yet been introduced, and there were plans for other badge-engineered derivatives to follow later.

A Vanden Plas 1800 and an Estate

Among the plans for derivatives of ADO17 was one to create a Vanden Plas model. In the BMC hierarchy, Vanden Plas (a formerly independent coachbuilder that had been bought out by Austin in 1947) was the name applied to top luxury models. For its first decade in Austin ownership, Vanden Plas had built special limousines on the Austin A135 chassis, but from 1958 BMC chose to apply the name to luxury models based on mainstream production cars. By the early 1960s, there were Vanden Plas derivatives of the big Farina saloons, which were sold with the Princess name, and from 1963, there was a remarkable compact luxury model called the Vanden Plas Princess 1100 which was based on the ADO16 front-wheel-drive saloon.

It was therefore no surprise that the 1800 should have been put forward as a candidate for Vanden Plas to work their magic. According to the Vanden Plas Owners' Club, an Austin 1800 was used as the basis of a prototype in March 1965. The front end was completely reworked, losing the bright metal headlamp surround panels of the original and gaining auxiliary lamps set into the front panel next to the characteristic Princess grille. Combined sidelamp and indicator units, as used on the Princess 1100 and the Vanden Plas 4-litre R, helped to reinforce the family look.

Above: The Vanden Plas proposal looked smart but that front end was not altogether happy; the peak-like feature above the headlamps did not really work.

Left: The 1800 shape adapted well to an estate, and made economical use of the Wolseley rear lights, too.

The rear treatment was unfortunately rather less successful, with extended wings, tail lights from the 4-litre R, and a raised boot lid with a sharply angled edge that contrasted with the pleasantly rounded lines elsewhere. Painted Dark Green and upholstered with Champagne Beige leather, it must have been most attractive (the surviving pictures are unfortunately all black and white). However, the design went no further, apparently because the car looked too similar to the standard ADO17 saloon. Vanden Plas would nevertheless be called on to try again a few years later.

The Vanden Plas derivative was not the only experimental ADO17 in this period. A picture exists of an estate-car 1800, probably a running prototype rather than a studio mock-up, and its dummy registration plate of AUS 1966 suggests it was either built in 1966 or intended as a 1966 model. The car in the picture has an extended roofline and enlarged rear side windows, with what appears to be a large top-hinged hatchback. To allow the hatch to open down to bumper level, it has Wolseley 18/85 vertical tail lights on the corners. The concept was good – and the success of Crayford's 1800 hatchback conversion (see Chapter 7) suggests that it might have proved successful, but the project was cancelled for two reasons. One was that it would have harmed sales of the existing estate models based on the 1.6-litre Farina saloons, and the other was that an 1800 hatchback would have been too similar to the planned ADO14 model, which later became the Austin Maxi.

The Morris Models

BMC's Morris dealers received their 1800s from March 1966, which certainly improved the ADO17's chances in the marketplace. But there were no surprises: to all intents and purposes, the cars were exactly the same as the Austin types already on sale. Even the showroom price was the same. They had Morris badges and a different radiator grille and, for those who looked closely enough, there was also a minor difference in the tail lights. The Morris versions came to a rounded point at their outer ends, while the Austin ones had a truncated end. No doubt the difference was a result of using different suppliers for the Austin and Morris assembly lines.

Behind the scenes, some work was being done to improve the 1800's appeal. There was an abortive facelift proposal during 1966, which fell a long way short of achieving what was needed. Modified gearshift cables introduced for all models when the Morris arrived cured difficult engagement of first and third gears in cold weather, and then in May a modification to the front seat mountings increased the rake and improved comfort a little.

For the 1967 models introduced in September 1966, higher-geared steering further improved the driving experience, bringing just 3.75 turns of the wheel between locks instead of the original 4.2 turns. From early 1967, a centre panel was added to break up the wide expanse of parcels shelf, containing an ashtray and a cubby box. Then from June 1967 there was a further suite of modifications, which were not formally notified to the press – probably to avoid attracting column inches that BMC preferred to see devoted to the new Wolseley derivative of the ADO17 that was released at the same time. Front bucket seats replaced the original split bench, the heater controls were repositioned more accessibly,

The Morris 1800 was exactly the same car as the Austin, but with different badges. A large Morris badge on a slatted grille certainly made it stand out.

The engine, too, was the same, but the Morris versions carried appropriate identification on their top covers. The side-mounted radiator is very apparent here.

and the facia gained a cheering strip of walnut veneer that was, of course, plastic rather than wood. A final and long-overdue specification change came in September 1967 in time for the 1968 model year, when power-assisted steering was made an extra-cost option for the Austin and Morris models.

TECHNICAL SPECIFICATIONS – AUSTIN AND MORRIS 1800 MK I

Engine:
Four-cylinder OHV B-series, mounted transversely
1798cc (80.26mm bore x 88.9mm stroke)
SU HS6 carburettor
8.2:1 compression ratio (6.8:1 available for export)
84bhp at 5300rpm
99lb ft at 2100rpm

Transmission:
Four-speed all-synchromesh manual gearbox; gear ratios 3.29:1, 2.22:1, 1.38:1, 1.00:1, reverse 3.08:1
Optional three-speed Borg Warner automatic; gear ratios 2.39:1, 1.45:1, 1.00:1, reverse 2.09:1
Final drive ratio 3.882:1 (4.19:1 on early Austin models and available for export thereafter)

Suspension:
Front suspension with twin wishbones and Hydrolastic units
Rear suspension with trailing arms, Hydrolastic units, and (to September 1965 only) anti-roll bar
Front and rear suspension interconnected through Hydrolastic system

Steering and Brakes:
Rack-and-pinion steering, with optional power assistance from September 1967
Front disc brakes (9.28in diameter) and rear drums (9in x 1.75in) with servo assistance

Wheels and Tyres:
13in wheels with 4.5in rims and 175 x 13 tyres

Dimensions and Weights:

Overall length	161.2in
Overall width	67in
Overall height	55.5in
Wheelbase	106in
Front track	56in
Rear track	55.5in
Weight	2645lb approx., unladen

Performance

Maximum speed	90mph
0–60mph	17.1 sec
Fuel consumption	24mpg

The Wolseley 18/85

BMC had never had the courage on its formation in the 1950s to streamline its dealerships. The dealers had, quite rightly, argued that they had spent many years encouraging loyalty to the marques for which they held a franchise. BMC's reaction to this was to create slightly different versions of each of its new products to suit different marques, a process that was somewhat derisively described as badge engineering.

A Riley derivative of the ADO17 was considered, but in the end the only marque that was chosen to receive a special version was Wolseley, and the model was named in the Wolseley tradition as an 18/85. The 18 represented its 1.8-litre engine, and the 85 indicated that engine's (approximately) 85bhp output. Buyers with long memories might have remembered that there had been an earlier Wolseley 18/85, a saloon model based on a Morris that was available in the years on either side of the Second World War. In the BMC catalogues, the new 18/85 replaced the Farina-styled Wolseley 6/110, although there was a decent overlap of a year during which both cars were available together. This allowed buyers to get used to the idea that the latest big Wolseley had only four cylinders rather than the more prestigious six of the older car.

The BMC styling team did make the car distinctive. They developed a proper Wolseley front end, with the marque's traditional grille and illuminated badge, and at the rear they designed some different tail lights that were vertical rather than horizontal. Wheels were given special trims with the Wolseley W embossed in the centre, and there were additional chrome trims and rubber-faced over-riders. The side repeater indicators were more ornate teardrop-shaped items than on the Austin and Morris models. The interior was given a wooden facia panel and traditional round instruments instead of the modernistic strip type on the Austin and Morris models. Pleated leather upholstery was accompanied by pile carpets, and reclining front seats were made available as an optional extra; Wolseley buyers also got an electric screen-wash system.

This 1968 Wolseley 18/85 has a winged-W mascot that was not part of the original specification. (SG2012, CC by 2.0)

To complete its luxury specification, the 18/85 had power-assisted steering as standard, and became the first of the ADO17 models to have an automatic gearbox – which was nevertheless an extra-cost option. That gearbox was of course made by Borg Warner, and was a three-speed type that was driven from the crankshaft by a Morse Hy-Vo chain rather than a set of gears. Its control lever was on the steering column, to the driver's right.

That was as far as the development budget would stretch, however. The engine remained unchanged, with the same 84bhp as in the Austin and Morris models. With the automatic gearbox, acceleration was just a little slower than in the manual cars, but it was all in keeping with the dignified air that went with the Wolseley marque. Nobody complained when the 18/85 was introduced in March 1967 with a price premium of about 18 per cent over its Austin 1800 sibling. The base price of £1,040 was inflated by £95 if the buyer ordered an automatic gearbox, but the car sold steadily for just over two years until it was replaced by a revised Mk II model in summer 1969.

Above: The Wosleley 18/85 was readily identified by its front-end details, which lent a certain elegance to the ADO17 shape. Clear here are the Wolseley logo on the wheel trims and the rubber-faced over-riders.

Right: A redesign at the rear gave the Wolseley models a neat set of rear lights, as well as Wolseley identification badges and some additional bright trim.

Above: The Wolseley of course had the same spacious interior as the Austin and Morris models, in this case enhanced by wood on the facia and leather on the seats.

Left: The Wolseley models were distinguished by elongated teardrop-shaped side repeater lamps.

The Wolseley rear light units were quite different from those on the Austin and Morris models, being oriented vertically rather than horizontally.

TECHNICAL SPECIFICATIONS – WOLSELEY 18/85 MK I

Engine:
1798cc (80.26mm bore x 88.9mm stroke) B-series four-cylinder, mounted transversely
85bhp at 5300rpm
99lb ft at 2100rpm

Transmission:
Four-speed all-synchromesh manual gearbox; gear ratios 3.29:1, 2.22:1, 1.38:1, 1.00:1, reverse 3.08:1
Optional three-speed Borg Warner automatic; gear ratios 2.39:1, 1.45:1, 1.00:1, reverse 2.09:1
Final drive ratio 3.882:1

Suspension:
Front suspension with twin wishbones and Hydrolastic units
Rear suspension with trailing arms and Hydrolastic units
Front and rear suspension interconnected through Hydrolastic system

Steering and Brakes:
Rack-and-pinion steering with standard power assistance
Front disc brakes and rear drums

Wheels and Tyres:
13in wheels with 175 x 13 tyres

Dimensions and Weights:

Overall length	166.1in
Overall width	67in
Overall height	55.5in
Wheelbase	106in
Front track	56in
Rear track	55.5in
Weight	2576lb approx., unladen

Performance:

Maximum speed	90mph
0–60mph	18.0 sec
Fuel consumption	22mpg

THE 1967 PININFARINA 1800

When the coachbuilder Pininfarina decided to build an advanced aerodynamic saloon to display at the Turin Motor Show in 1967, his choice of host car fell on a BMC 1800. It was an interesting selection, perhaps influenced by the fact that the car was, mechanically, an advanced front-wheel-drive design that would complement the forward-looking ethos of the Pininfarina concept. Perhaps the Italian design house wanted to maintain good relations with BMC, which had been a decent customer over the previous decade. Perhaps both considerations influenced the choice.

The design was known as the Pininfarina Berlina Aerodynamica and, as that name suggests, its primary focus was on aerodynamics. It was the work of Leonardo Fioravanti, who had been with the Pininfarina studio since 1964 and who was fascinated by aerodynamic design and in particular by the theory of the cut-off Kamm tail, which this design had. The car was a remarkable two-box design with a sleek and streamlined shape that anticipated (and undoubtedly influenced) design trends of the 1970s. It was also a convincing demonstration of the Italian design house's talents.

The project began over the summer of 1967 with a wooden model. Pininfarina asked BMC for an 1800 to convert, and car number 82605 (perhaps only part-built) arrived in Turin on 10 August 1967. Working with characteristic speed, the Italian design house had turned it into a show car in time for the opening of the Turin Motor Show on 1 November.

Motor magazine described it as 'a remarkable exercise on the unlikely base of an Austin 1800. One only has to look at the original to see that this must be the transformation of the decade.' Issigonis was excited by it, but George Harriman made clear that BMC were not about to take it up. That did not stop Pininfarina trying. The company presented a report on the car to BMC in December, and then tried again in 1968 with a similar design based on an 1100. But by then, BMC had been absorbed into British Leyland, and the new management had no appetite for outsourcing design to Italian coachbuilders. The 1800-based car was shipped to Longbridge, where it was used for a time by Harry Webster, the Austin-Morris chief engineer under British Leyland, and acquired the nickname of 'Yellow Peril'. It subsequently disappeared.

Pininfarina's saloon concept built on an 1800 floorpan was breathtaking for 1967, but was too futuristic for BMC management.

3

Mk II Models, 1968–72

Four years into its production, the ADO17 range received a facelift. In broad terms, the idea was to refresh the car and add new appeal that would keep sales going for a few more years, although by this stage it must have been clear that a simple facelift was not going to enable the car to reach the sales figures that had earlier been predicted for it. The first of the new cars were introduced in May 1968 and were known, rather prosaically, as Mk II models. There were only Austin and Morris derivatives at first, and the existing Wolseley 18/85 remained on sale alongside them for well over a year before it, too, was upgraded to the Mk II specification. All these changes, of course, had been planned before BMC was subsumed into British Leyland in January 1968.

In fact, the facelift took place in two stages, so giving British Leyland two bites at the publicity cherry. The first stage introduced Mk II versions of the familiar Austin and

The main recognition point of the Mk II Austin 1800 from this angle was its new grille. (De Facto, CC by 4.0)

Above: Recognition was much easier from behind. The Mk II models had reshaped rear wings with vertical lights, which tended to make the car look less wide than it really was, and there was a plate badge on the left of the boot lid. Automatic models, like this 1969 example, had a script badge on the right. (De Facto, CC by 4.0)

Below: Once again, the Morris versions had a different grille and, once again, it carried a prominent Morris badge. This is a 1970 car. (De Facto, CC by SA 2.5)

Morris models, and the second stage broadened the range by adding 1800S models with additional performance. This second stage coincided with the Motor Show in October 1968, and it was characterised by yet another of the strange arrangements with Austin and Morris dealers that were supposed to ensure even-handed treatment. This time, Morris dealers received the S models first, and Austin dealers did not get theirs until a year later.

The Mk II Changes

The cosmetic changes were quite limited but also quite effective, at least in distinguishing the Mk II models from the earlier cars. In practice, Austin and Morris variants looked even more alike than they had before, but new grilles kept them distinct. The Austin version now had more prominent bars, though still with a small marque badge, and the Morris version had different bars and a much-larger Morris emblem in the centre.

Both cars shared the changes at the rear, where the rear wings lost their downturn and were sharpened up, providing the shape for new vertical tail-lamp clusters. There were new plate badges on the left of the boot lid, the same shape in each case but with identification

Rear badges made clear that these were Mk II models. This is the Morris version.

The underbonnet view of this Morris 1800 Mk II shows few differences from that of the Mk I car pictured in the previous chapter – but there were some differences in the position of the ancillaries around the engine.

as appropriate to the car. Less obvious unless Mk I and Mk II cars were viewed side by side was that the Mk IIs had larger 14-inch wheels with narrower tyres – a change supposedly introduced to lighten the steering rather than for any cosmetic benefit.

There were limited revisions inside the passenger cabin, too. Here, the Mk II dashboard gained a wooden strip, a padded knee-roll on the edge of the parcels shelf, and rocker switches instead of the toggle switches of the Mk I cars. The handbrake was repositioned, and was now released by a trigger rather than by twisting it. Typical of the times was the replacement of leather upholstery by Ambla, a vinyl leather-cloth material.

Then there were some minor mechanical changes as well. A higher compression ratio, cylinder head changes that improved breathing, and lightweight pistons combined to add

It was perhaps only a strip of wood veneer – but that alteration to the dashboard did help to make the Mk II version look less plain than the original. A central 'cubby' also added character, and of course there were changes to the door trims as well.

The strip-type speedometer remained on the Mk II models, as seen here on a Morris 1800.

The spacious rear seat remained unchanged, although upholstery was now in vinyl rather than leather. This is a Morris.

a couple of extra brake horsepower. The manual-gearbox models gained a higher second gear ratio. Power-assisted steering, already introduced as an option on the last of the Mk I cars, remained available, but still as an option for the Austin and Morris models (it was standard on the Wolseley 18/85). There were also changes to the suspension, where Slipflex bearings in the suspension arms replaced the roller bearings used on Mk I models, mainly as a cost-saving measure.

At the October 1968 Motor Show, the 1800 De Luxe model with manual gearbox was listed at £998 15*s* 0*d*, of which £218 15*s* 0*d* was Purchase Tax.

A HYBRID SPECIFICATION

The changeover to the Mk II specification was not a completely clean one. Some late Mk I models (especially Wolseleys) were built with the Mk II engine (coded 18H), 14-inch wheels, and interior modifications such as the new handbrake lever, interior door-release handles, and window winders.

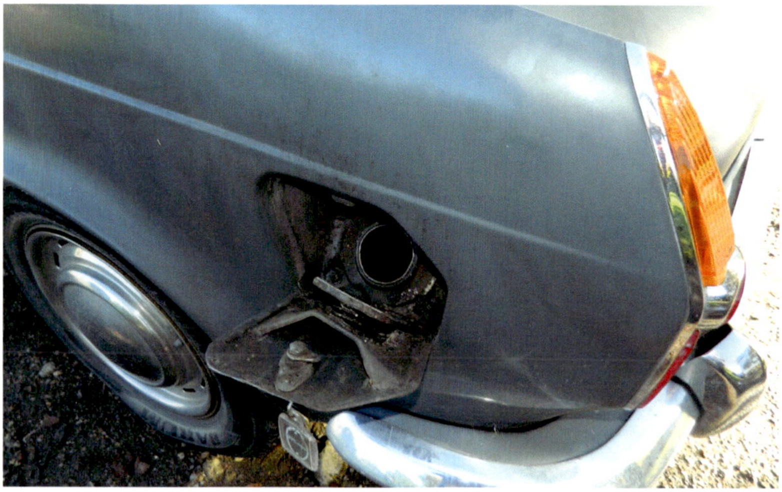

The lockable fuel filler cap in the rear wing had a neat arrangement.

The bonnet release on the Mk II was still this catch, accessible from outside the car. An internal release would be fitted on the Mk III models.

The S Models

The main point of the S models was to add higher-performance variants to the range without frightening the more conservative buyers who made up a large section of the 1800's audience. It was relatively easy to do: BMC had engaged Daniel Richmond of Downton Engineering to work on the cylinder head, and by raising the compression ratio and fitting twin carburettors, an MGB camshaft, and a three-branch tubular exhaust manifold, the engine was persuaded to deliver 96bhp. That made the 1800S a near-100mph car.

Acceleration improved, too, thanks to increased engine torque, and to keep everything in check when needed the S models came with bigger three-piston Girling disc brake calipers on the front wheels. Morris (and Austin from 1969) played to the gallery a little by adding an S badge on the boot lid and, when the Austin 1800S became available in 1969, giving both models a stripe of contrasting colour down each side. Yet, despite a new 120mph speedometer, and despite the absence of an automatic option, the 1800S models were not really any more sporty than the standard 1800s; quicker, maybe, but handling was unchanged, and so was the steering.

The Morris 1800S cost £1,049 17*s* 3*d* at the time of the Motor Show in October 1968, and of that £229 17*s* 3*d* was Purchase Tax. In January 1969, a Morris 1800S was the subject of a comparison test with the latest Renault 16TS in *Car* magazine, whose testers admitted that they had 'a much softer spot for the car than we used to have, but there is still that gearchange and that driving position to hold against it'. The 1800S was, they admitted, 'a straight answer to those who wanted to see it [the ADO17] with more power. But we would have liked to feel more of it at the bottom end, to get the car off the mark quicker.' It went better than the single-carburettor 1800, but 'nobody should fool himself into thinking that the S variant is a sparkling performer, and if he is interested in bottom-end pull for, say, caravan towing, he may be better off with the standard car'.

Above: A contrasting side stripe made the 1800-S model stand out. This is the Morris version.

Right: The interest here is in the carburettors; two of them rather than one indicate that this engine is in an Austin 1800-S.

TECHNICAL SPECIFICATIONS – AUSTIN AND MORRIS 1800 MK II AND MK II S

Engine (1800):
1798cc (80.26mm bore x 88.9mm stroke) B-series four-cylinder, mounted transversely
Single SU HS6 carburettor
Compression ratio 9.1:1
86bhp at 5300rpm
101lb ft at 3000rpm

Engine (1800S):
1798cc (80.26mm bore x 88.9mm stroke) B-series four-cylinder, mounted transversely
Two SU HS6 carburettors
Compression ratio 9.5:1
96bhp at 5700rpm
106lb ft at 3000rpm

Transmission:
Four-speed all-synchromesh manual gearbox; gear ratios 3.29:1, 2.06:1, 1.38:1, 1.00:1, reverse 3.08:1
Optional three-speed Borg Warner automatic (not available on S models); gear ratios 2.39:1, 1.45:1, 1.00:1, reverse 2.09:1
Final drive ratio 3.882:1; 4.19:1 available for export

Suspension:
Front suspension with upper and lower arms, locating tie-rods and Hydrolastic units
Rear suspension with trailing arms and Hydrolastic units
Front and rear suspension interconnected through Hydrolastic system

Steering and Brakes:
Rack-and-pinion steering with standard power assistance
Front disc brakes (9.28in diameter) and rear drums (9in x 1.75in); three-piston front calipers on S models

Wheels and Tyres:
14in wheels with 4.5in rims and 165 x 14 tyres

Dimensions and Weights:

Overall length	166.1in
Overall width	67in
Overall height	55.5in
Wheelbase	106in
Front track	56in

Rear track	55.5in
Weight	3025lb approx. (1800S)

Performance:

Maximum speed	93mph; S model 99mph
0–60mph	16.3 sec; S model 13.7 sec
Fuel consumption	27mpg; S model 22mpg

The Mk II Wolseley 18/85 and 18/85S

Nobody is quite sure why Wolseley buyers had to wait an extra twelve months before the Mk II 18/85 appeared, but when it did arrive in May 1969 it incorporated all the chassis changes that had already been made to the Austin and Morris variants of ADO17. It also had a few special differences of its own.

On the outside, the car was unchanged except for a 'II' badge on the boot lid. It still had the special Wolseley grille and front-end details, the Wolseley-branded hubcaps, and the vertical tail lights. However, there were some valuable changes inside the passenger compartment. The seats had been reshaped to give greater comfort, and the front pair were now recliners as standard. The redesigned door trims now had wooden top fillets to add a little more to the luxury ambience, and the facia now had rocker-type switches instead of the earlier toggle type. On the doors, the flat plastic handles from the Austin and Morris models replaced the earlier chromed type. Buyers paid £1,224 for the Mk II model, and an extra £101 if they wanted the optional automatic gearbox.

For those who wanted a little more performance as well, September 1969 brought the Mk II S derivative of the 18/85. This simply added the more powerful twin-carburettor engine that had been announced in the Austin 1800S in July, and of course added a little to the price as well. Both the standard 18/85 and the S version could be ordered with a Borg Warner automatic gearbox, adding still more to the price. The S announced its extra cost and performance with a side strip that contrasted with the main body colour, but still retained its distinctive teardop shaped side repeater lamps. There was also, of course, an S badge on the tail. Both versions of the Mk II Wolseley remained popular until 1972, when they gave way to the new six-cylinder Wolseley Six.

The Wolseley 18/85 was still quite different to look at from the other ADO17 variants, but it was not as easy to tell that it was a Mk II model.

TECHNICAL SPECIFICATIONS – WOLSELEY 18/85 MK II AND 18/85S

Engine (18/85):
1798cc (80.26mm bore x 88.9mm stroke) B-series four-cylinder, mounted transversely
Single SU HS6 carburettor
86bhp at 5300rpm
101lb ft at 3000rpm

Engine (18/85S):
1798cc (80.26mm bore x 88.9mm stroke) B-series four-cylinder, mounted transversely
Two SU HS6 carburettors
96bhp at 5700rpm
106lb ft at 3000rpm

Transmission:
Four-speed all-synchromesh manual gearbox; gear ratios 3.29:1, 2.06:1, 1.38:1, 1.00:1, reverse 3.08:1
Optional three-speed Borg Warner automatic; gear ratios 2.39:1, 1.45:1, 1.00:1, reverse 2.09:1
Final drive ratio 3.882:1

Suspension:
Front suspension with twin wishbones and Hydrolastic units
Rear suspension with trailing arms and Hydrolastic units
Front and rear suspension interconnected through Hydrolastic system

Steering and Brakes:
Rack-and-pinion steering with standard power assistance
Front disc brakes and rear drums

Wheels and Tyres:
14in wheels with 165 x 14 tyres

Dimensions and Weights:

Overall length	166.1in	Wheelbase	106in
Overall width	67in	Front track	56in
Overall height	55.5in	Rear track	55.5in

Weight	2624lb approx., unladen

Performance:

Maximum speed	97mph; S model 99mph
0–60mph	15.2 sec; S model 13.7 sec
Fuel consumption	24mpg; S model 22mpg

A Second Vanden Plas Attempt

As Chapter 2 explains, BMC had asked Vanden Plas to put forward ideas for a luxurious and upmarket 1800 derivative that could be badged as a Vanden Plas Princess, but the coachbuilder's first attempt had been unsatisfactory. The idea then lay dormant for a few years, until it was taken up again under British Leyland in 1970.

This time, Vanden Plas were given a very early example of the Australian X6 bodyshell (see Chapter 5) to work on. This was probably a UK-built prototype, and whether they had specifically requested it or not is simply unclear. They grafted on a new front end, apparently using UK-production wings and headlamp surrounds but also adding typical Vanden Plas features, such as the expected large grille and auxiliary driving lamps set into the front panel. They added new tail lights and 'Vanden Plas Princess' badges, and of course their trademark hubcaps with the ornate 'P' for Princess centre badge.

The car that resulted was a very happy compromise, its four-light Australian-style bodyshell helping it to stand out from the standard UK-built ADO17s of the time and its distinctive front end giving it just the right amount of upmarket Vanden Plas appeal. This one was painted in a most attractive metallic silver, complemented by tan leather upholstery. It was registered for the road (as AOB 823K) in August 1971 and was generally considered an aesthetic success. However, sales of the ADO17 range were still low, and British Leyland clearly decided not to spend the money on putting a more expensive derivative into production. The Vanden Plas 1800 therefore remained unique. Later sold off, it has fortunately remained in enthusiast hands and still exists.

The second attempt by Vanden Plas to create a Princess from the 1800 was much more successful. This is the prototype car, which is now in preservation. (Andrew Bone, CCA 2.0)

The reshaped rear quarters made the car look longer and more elegant than a standard 1800 – which was exactly what customers expected from a Vanden Plas model. (Andrew Bone, CCA 2.0)

The rear three-quarter view makes make clear that the Vanden Plas prototype was created from an Australian-type bodyshell.

The Sales Picture

Despite the facelift and despite the availability of models with power steering and higher performance, sales of the ADO17 range did not improve. The 1800s simply soldiered on, plugging their own gap in the market while a variety of other British Leyland models filled the public need for a 1.5-litre saloon. In mid-1972, production of the Mk II models was brought to an end and a final, Mk III, range was introduced.

4

Mk III Models and Sixes, 1972–75

Both the Mk I and the Mk II variants of ADO17 had been conceived and developed under BMC management, but the final phase of the range's life was the result of British Leyland thinking. Central to it was the introduction of a six-cylinder engine for top models, and these replaced the twin-carburettor S models. Alongside these, the single-carburettor Austin and Morris 1800s continued as Mk III types, but there was no longer a four-cylinder Wolseley derivative; the 18/85 model was dropped.

The revised models were announced in March 1972, looking very much like the Mk II cars that they replaced. The Austin and Morris variants shared a new radiator grille, this time finished in matt black and highlighted by slim horizontal chrome bars. Over-riders disappeared altogether, giving a cleaner look (and no doubt saving a few pennies on the manufacturing cost as well). As was happening elsewhere in the British Leyland model ranges, little plate badges with the blue British Leyland symbol now became standard at the bottom of each front wing just behind the wheelarch.

Looking very smart in dark blue, this is a January 1973 Mk III Austin 1800. The new grille is partially obscured behind all those badges, but the small British Leyland badge is clear on the front wing behind the wheelarch. (Charles 01, GNU Free Documentation Licence)

Above: The new grille and the darkened headlamp surrounds are clear on this July 1975 Morris 2200, painted in a colour so typical of its time. (Charles 01, CC by 4.0)

Below: This rear view of a six-cylinder Austin shows the optional styled steel wheels and Austin 2200 badges. It is an automatic model, and has the same script badge on the right as its predecessors. Next to that, the small badge is that of the supplying garage in the Netherlands. (Joost J Bakker, CC by 2.0)

The interior overhaul was more comprehensive. The cars took on a very plain wooden facia, with angled sections that prevented it from looking like a featureless slab of wood. The six-cylinder cars gained round instrument dials, face-level air vents were now integrated into the design, and the handbrake was finally located in its conventional position on the floor between the two front seats. There was a redesigned steering wheel, too, its two padded spokes being more consciously styled than those of the earlier cars. Out of sight, there was also an improvement to the gear change, which lost its cable linkage in favour of rod operation – just as had been done for the Austin Maxi a year earlier.

The Six-Cylinder Engine

The new six-cylinder engine was not quite as new as it appeared to British buyers in 1972, because it had actually been available in the Australian-built Austin X6 range (see Chapter 5) since 1970. When it arrived in the British-built cars, it was therefore an engine that was well tried and tested in harsher conditions than were normally encountered in the UK.

The six-cylinder engine was often called the E6, to distinguish it from its four-cylinder E-series sibling. BMC had drawn that up shortly before it became part of British Leyland but, because British Leyland were in charge by the time it was introduced, the engine has generally become known as a Leyland E-series.

The E-series was designed from the start as a transverse engine for BMC's front-wheel-drive cars, and was always intended to have both four-cylinder and six-cylinder variants that could be machined on the same tooling. However, it was the four-cylinder that was prepared first, with a nominal 1.5-litre size, and this engine entered production in both Britain and Australia during 1969. In Britain, it became the power unit of the Austin Maxi,

The six-cylinder engine's extra length made it necessary to relocate the radiator at the front of the engine bay. That angled scoop ensured that the twin carburettors received enough air to do their job.

while in Australia it went into local derivatives of the ADO16 range (better known as the Austin and Morris 1100).

In fact, the 1.5-litre size was not the smallest capacity originally planned. BMC had wanted a 1.3-litre engine, but it became clear early on that this would offer only minimal benefits over the 1.3-litre size that was being developed from the older A-series engine at the same time. The six-cylinder with the bore and stroke of the 1.3-litre E-series would have given a 2.0-litre nominal capacity – but it was never developed.

It was the Australians who took the lead with the eventual six-cylinder E-series because they needed such an engine to make the ADO17 competitive in their domestic market. Australians expected a car with the physical dimensions of the 1800 to have considerably more power, and so it was Australian engineers who picked up the plan for a six-cylinder E-series and carried it through. In tandem with UK engineers, they developed the engine from the bore and stroke dimensions of the 1.5-litre four-cylinder E-series that was already in production, which gave a swept volume of 2227cc. The E6 engine entered production in Australia during 1970.

The characteristics of this six-cylinder engine were interesting. Its block had to be short for the intended transverse installation in these front-wheel-drive cars, and that both limited the bore size and persuaded the designers to dispense with a water jacket between each pair of cylinders. The required capacity was achieved by a long stroke, and in an OHC design with the traditional BMC gearbox-in-sump layout, that made for a very tall engine. Even then, the engine could only be accommodated in the ADO17 engine bay by moving the radiator from the side to the front, and that part of the installation was developed by Smith Industries, who of course supplied the radiators.

At Longbridge, the engine was able to share machine tooling with the four cylinder E-series, and the two engines also shared a number of components: valve gear, pistons, con rods, and timing gear were all among the common elements.

The dashboard was redesigned for the Mk III models. Though fairly simple in style, it was quite effective.

The padded steering-wheel spokes were very much a piece of 1970s design. This is a six-cylinder car, with the blanking piece for the optional radio next to the choke control in the centre.

Six-cylinder models had a different type of upholstery from the 1800s, with a slightly more sporty appearance.

Six-Cylinder Austin and Morris

The six-cylinder Austin and Morris variants were both released at the same time and were both badged as 2200 models. They could be had with either the old four-speed gearbox (with a larger-diameter clutch than on the 1800) or the three-speed Borg Warner automatic, and were identically priced. There really was no longer any reason for choosing one version over the other, except for marque loyalty or simply the convenience of a nearby dealership.

Perhaps most surprising was that there was nothing obvious to indicate that these were the six-cylinder models and therefore carried greater prestige than the visually identical four-cylinder 1800s. The insides of the headlamp recesses now had a matt-black finish to match the grille, but this was probably too subtle for most people. There certainly was a badge – just one – on the boot lid that described each car as a 2200 type and also bore the marque name. Otherwise, there was nothing. Arguably, British Leyland had taken traditional British discretion beyond the bounds of business sense.

However, the six-cylinder cars could be ordered with styled and painted Rostyle pressed steel wheels as an option. Not available on the four-cylinder cars, these gave a slightly more modern and slightly more sporty look to a design that was by now even more out of step with European design trends than it had been when first released eight years earlier in 1964. They were also distinguished on the inside by seat wearing surfaces with a basket-weave pattern that was quite different from the pleating of the 1800 models.

The biggest barrier to success for these six-cylinder cars was that customer expectations of cars in the 2-litre size class had changed. The Rover 2000 and Triumph 2000 that had been introduced in 1963 – a year before ADO17 and half a decade before British Leyland was

This November 1972 Morris 2200 is wearing the optional Rostyle styled and painted steel wheels.

formed – pioneered the idea of a compact, sleek and quite sporty 'executive' car, and the Austin and Morris 2200 models were none of those things. That did not bother a proportion of probably family-oriented customers, but it must certainly have deterred more than a few potential buyers.

Wolseley Six

The Wolseley models were now positioned very clearly at the top of the ADO17 range, and were also given the rather more prestigious-sounding name of Wolseley Six. They had most of the usual exterior distinguishing features, and the same blacked-out headlamp recesses as the other six-cylinder models but, again like the rest of the range, their bumpers no longer carried over-riders. The same styled and painted wheels could be had as optional extras, too.

Inside the passenger cabin, the Wolseley Six was as plush as buyers had come to expect from the marque, with leather upholstery instead of the vinyl of the other cars and a not entirely convincing burr-walnut veneer on the dashboard. The dashboard contained a clock, and the wood veneer was extended to the ashtrays in the backs of the front seats, where ruched map pockets were another small touch that made a worthwhile difference.

That British Leyland had got the six-cylinder Wolseley right became clearer as sales mounted up, and over its three-year production run it would go on to become the best-selling car in the Mk III range. This, almost certainly, was what persuaded its makers to develop a Wolseley derivative of the ADO71 '18/22' wedge-shaped range that replaced it in 1975. Sadly, that would be the last ever Wolseley, as it disappeared from the range after a few months when a rethink of marketing strategy removed the focus on marque names and placed it firmly on the brand name of Princess.

This 1972 Wolseley Six appears to have lost the dark shading from its headlamp surrounds. A subtle difference on these cars was that the elongated teardrop side repeater lamps had been repositioned below the pinstripe on the wing. (De Facto, CC by 2.5)

Above: This rear view of the same car confirms that it is the six-cylinder model, and that it has an automatic gearbox. (De Facto, CC by 2.5)

Below: As always, the Wolseley interior was just a little more plush than the Austin and Morris types, and the figured wood dash and seatback map pockets are clear in this picture.

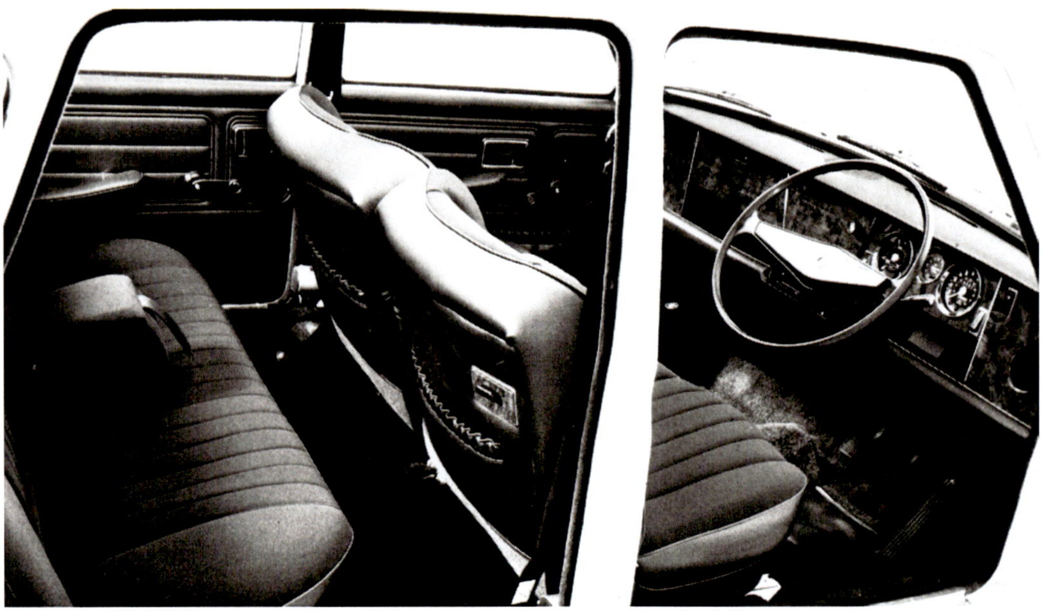

TECHNICAL SPECIFICATIONS – AUSTIN AND MORRIS 1800 MK III

Engine:
1798cc (80.26mm bore x 88.9mm stroke) B-series four-cylinder, mounted transversely
Single SU HS6 carburettor
Compression ratio 9.1:1
86bhp at 5300rpm
101lb ft at 3000rpm

Transmission:
Four-speed all-synchromesh manual gearbox; gear ratios 3.29:1, 2.06:1, 1.38:1, 1.00:1, reverse 3.08:1
Optional three-speed Borg Warner automatic; gear ratios 2.39:1, 1.45:1, 1.00:1, reverse 2.09:1
Final drive ratio 3.882:1; 4.19:1 available for export

Suspension:
Front suspension with upper and lower arms, locating tie-rods and Hydrolastic units
Rear suspension with trailing arms and Hydrolastic units
Front and rear suspension interconnected through Hydrolastic system

Steering and Brakes:
Rack-and-pinion steering with optional power assistance
Front disc brakes (9.28in diameter) and rear drums (9in x 1.75in)

Wheels and Tyres:
14in wheels with 4.5in rims and 165 x 14 tyres

Dimensions and Weights:

Overall length	166.1in
Overall width	67in
Overall height	55.5in
Wheelbase	106in
Front track	56in
Rear track	55.5in
Weight	2547lb (kerb weight)

Performance:

Maximum speed	93mph
0–60mph	16.3 sec
Fuel consumption	27mpg

TECHNICAL SPECIFICATIONS – AUSTIN AND MORRIS 2200, WOLSELEY SIX

Engine:
2227cc (76.2mm bore x 81.3mm stroke) E-series six-cylinder, mounted transversely
Two SU HS6 carburettors
Compression ratio 9.0:1
110bhp at 5250rpm
126lb ft at 3500rpm

Transmission:
Four-speed all-synchromesh manual gearbox; gear ratios 3.29:1, 2.06:1, 1.38:1, 1.00:1, reverse 3.08:1
Optional three-speed Borg Warner automatic; gear ratios 2.39:1, 1.45:1, 1.00:1, reverse 2.09:1
Final drive ratio 3.882:1

Suspension:
Front suspension with upper and lower arms, locating tie-rods and Hydrolastic units
Rear suspension with trailing arms and Hydrolastic units
Front and rear suspension interconnected through Hydrolastic system

Steering and Brakes:
Rack-and-pinion steering with optional power assistance
Front disc brakes (9.7in diameter) and rear drums (9in x 1.75in)

Wheels and Tyres:
14in wheels with 4.5in rims and 165 x 14 tyres

Dimensions and Weights:

Overall length	166.1in
Overall width	67in
Overall height	55.5in
Wheelbase	106in
Front track	56in
Rear track	55.5in
Weight	2617lb (kerb weight)

Performance:

Maximum speed	104mph
0–60mph	13.1 sec
Fuel consumption	22mpg

Epilogue

With hindsight, it is not difficult to see why the ADO17 range never became the success its makers had anticipated when it was new. As Chapter 2 explains, the decision to use a 1.8-litre engine moved it out of the market sector for which it had originally been intended. It also encouraged its designer to make it a much larger car, with the result that its proportions were somewhat compromised. All this also left BMC, and later British Leyland, without the new 1.5-litre car that they wanted, so that the old BMC Farina models had to struggle on in the marketplace for several years beyond their natural sell-by date.

Yet buyers did appreciate its spacious passenger cabin, and in most cases that was enough to counter the disadvantages of its slightly strange driving position. Suspension comfort with the Hydrolastic system was excellent, and set the ADO17 above most other models in its class. Throughout its life, the car always retained a certain cachet that came from its advanced engineering specification.

Today, the 1800s and 2200s are few and far between. They have not become mainstream classic cars, but nevertheless have a strong and dedicated following of their own. They invariably attract interest at classic-car events, both for their nostalgia value and for their relative rarity. Enthusiasts are well served by three clubs, which can be found on the internet. All variants are catered for by the Landcrab Owners Club International (www.landcrab.net), while the Wolseley Owners Club (www.wolseleyownersclub.com) and the Wolseley Register (www.wolseleyregister.co.uk) obviously focus on the Wolseley variants as part of their wider Wolseley marque remit. There are also of course many Austin and Morris marque clubs around the world that welcome owners of ADO17s with these badges, and contact details can usually be found in the classic-car press.

A LEGACY ... OF SORTS

BMC began to develop the new 1.5-litre car that it had really wanted all along at about the time the ADO17 models reached the market. Development of this car was held up, partly because of financial problems in 1966–67, but it eventually emerged in April 1969 as the Austin Maxi. By then, of course, British Leyland rather than BMC was the name on the maker's masthead.

The Maxi's use of Issigonis' favoured engineering layout – front-wheel drive, transverse engines, and Hydrolastic suspension – was no great surprise, and nor was it a disappointment. However, what was disappointing was the decision to use the doors that had been designed for the 1800. This was done to save development and tooling costs, but it also fatally compromised the styling. Even so, as a result the Maxi kept the ADO17 flag flying in its own way until it was finally replaced in 1979.

Those doors had another legacy, too, as they were reused for the ADO61 3-litre cars that are described in Chapter 6.

In 1969, the Austin Maxi arrived to fill the 1.5-litre family saloon spot that the 1800 should have occupied. It came with the same front and rear doors, which emphasised the family resemblance but must have made life difficult for the styling team. (John Shepherd, CC by 2.0)

5

Aussies and Kiwis

The big front-wheel-drive BMC cars had their own special story Down Under, where they were first sold by BMC's Australian subsidiary in 1965. They were announced there on 22 November 1965, after a twelve-month test period to determine how they would stand up to Australian conditions. Despite the robust and rugged nature of the 1800, the Australians identified over forty areas where the ADO17 needed modifications.

They called for an increased ride height and a sump guard to make the car fit for rough country, stronger engine mountings, a heavier-duty clutch, sharper steering and a more progressive accelerator linkage. On the inside, they determined that Australian buyers would want more thickly padded seats with front recliners and safety belts as standard, armrests on the front doors, and better sealing against water and dust.

So it was that the first Australian cars were not quite the same as the ones sold in other countries, even though they were readily recognisable as ADO17s. They were Austin-badged 1800 models, not shipped out from the UK and locally modified but rather assembled at the BMC plant in Victoria Park, Sydney, using a combination of locally manufactured and imported components, and obviously incorporating all those changes that the early tests had recommended. The assembly lines were actually located in the building known as CAB1 (Car Assembly Building No 1), and before long production had reached around 1,000 cars a month.

The complete bodyshell was made in Australia, and in the beginning the engine and transmission were supplied from the UK as fully-built units. Automatic gearboxes always arrived fully built from Borg Warner in the UK, but the arrangements for the engine and manual gearbox changed quite early on so that they began to reach Australia from the UK in CKD form. The cylinder block, cylinder head, crankshaft and gearbox case all arrived fully machined ready for local assembly. Most other components were locally sourced in Australia, as assembly had to meet a local-manufacture percentage target that had been laid down in the Australian Federal Government's Local Content legislation.

So, for example, instead of the Girling brakes of the British-built cars, the Australian 1800s had Australian-made PBR (Paton's Brake Replacement) types. Later on, a production modification would see the handbrake repositioned between the front seats, thus anticipating the change on UK models by around four years. Further production changes

The Car of the Century? That was what Australian advertising called it, and this 1968 advertisement was designed to make it look as Australian and modern as the Sydney Opera House.

were intended to reduce manufacturing costs, and included the deletion of over-riders and the replacement of the single-piece rear bumpers by three-piece types.

Mk II models arrived in January 1969, a little after their introduction on the UK assembly lines. Local magazine *Modern Motor* perhaps hit the nail on the head with their comment that, 'if they'd only make the thing look as good as it really is, BMC would have the sales winner on their hands that they deserve – and need. But BMC have always underrated the importance today's market puts on styling.' Yet the 1800 continued to sell, the total figure for Australia being estimated at around 60,000 by the time the car was replaced in 1970; this figure includes the utes, which are described below.

Australian-built 1800s were exported to New Zealand, too, where the saloons were called the BMC 1800 Freeway. They had Austin grilles with a BMC badge; normal practice was for BMC models to carry Morris badging in New Zealand. The Freeway name was not new, but had been used for Australian-assembled versions of the A60 Farina range with a locally designed six-cylinder version of the B-series engine.

Above: This rare example is a BMC Freeway, the Australian-assembled version of the Austin 1800 that was exported to New Zealand. Note the BMC badge where the Austin one normally sat. (Riley, CC by 2.0)

Below: In this rear view of the same car, the special Freeway badge is clearly visible. (Riley, CC by 2.0)

The 1800 Utes

Meanwhile, Australian BMC dealers had been complaining that they had no models to compete in the utility market – an important one in Australia where a large pick-up was a vital necessity for outback farms. They claimed that lack of such a vehicle also had an impact on sales of BMC saloons, and some asked if they could sell Japanese-made pick-ups to compensate. The upshot of all this was that a design feasibility study was carried out, and it concluded that the ADO17 platform was the best to adapt as a utility because of its size and engine power. It would have to compete with big car-derived pick-ups from the Australian market leaders, who were Chrysler, Ford, and Holden.

BMC agreed that the Australian engineering team should design and develop this new model, which was allocated the project code YDO10. The YDO codes had been initiated in 1962 with the Morris Major Elite and were allocated to uniquely Australian models. (There was a matching Y code in uniquely Australian BMC part numbers.) Financial estimates were based on a sales figure of 10,000 units over three years at tooling costs of £250,000. Sadly, the Austin 1800 ute never sold anywhere near that number.

The Austin 1800 Ute was a uniquely Australian confection, a pick-up truck with an 1800 cab and front section. (Sicnag, CCA 2.0)

Above: The rear view in this publicity picture shows how the 1800 Utility had its own slim vertical tail lights to give as wide a tailgate opening as possible.

Right: The 1800 Ute was also available in chassis-cab form for special bodywork.

The idea was for YDO10 to be made available both as a chassis-cab (for local or DIY bodywork) and as a complete vehicle with 'ute' (pick-up) body. Initial calculations suggested that the rear suspension would need larger Hydrolastic displacers and a set of torsion bars to handle the half-ton load capacity that was planned. An interesting early proposal was for the gear lever on manual models to be moved outboard of the driver so that the middle passenger on a three-abreast bench seat would have full legroom. Sadly, both this and a proposed column gearchange were ruled out on cost grounds, although the 1800 utes did get their bench seat.

The YDO10 bodyshell with its platform rear was tooled for Australian manufacture and used the ADO17 underframe and front doors with a modified roof panel and a new cab rear panel. The first of these 1800 utes went on sale on 19 July 1968 and depended on the same combination of imported CKD and locally manufactured components as the contemporary 1800 saloons. The YDO10 utilities did not take on the Mk II specification until March 1969, and in this guise continued until 1970. Once again, there were exports to New Zealand, where the utes were badged as Morris 1800 types. Only about 2,000 utilities had been built by the time production ended, which was a rather disappointing result, and examples remained available in dealerships for some time after 1800 production ended.

SOME RARITIES

A few rarities were based on the Australian-built Austin 1800. One was a van, of which three or four are believed to have been built for the Royal Australian Navy from what were probably Mk I bodyshells. They appear not to have been built at Victoria Park but to have been specially converted by a commercial body builder, using a GRP roof panel and twin rear doors.

The second rarity was a camper van, which essentially used an 1800 front end and drivetrain with a camper back body. Supposedly three examples were built, one from a Mk I and the other two from Mk IIs.

Tasman and Kimberley

Meanwhile, BMC Australia had of course become BLMC Australia in 1968 after its UK parent company had merged with the Leyland Group. An early initiative was to determine ways of halting the decline in Australian sales, and to that end the Australian branch drew up a medium-term plan for new models that would be locally developed. The new cars were known as Model A (a small saloon) and Model B (a large one), and although the plans did not come to fruition as hoped, the Model B car did enter production in 1973 as the Leyland P76.

Production of these two new models was still some way off, and the company that had evolved into Leyland Australia urgently needed a six-cylinder model to make its mark on that booming sector of the market. The solution agreed was to develop a special derivative of ADO17, using a six-cylinder version of the four-cylinder E-series engine already being made in Australia for the Morris Nomad, a 1.5-litre hatchback derivative of the BMC 1100 range. Work had begun on this engine in the UK but, as explained in Chapter 4, the Australian engineers were the first to reach a production specification. The new Australian car was given the local development code of YDO13 and was planned to replace the 1800 altogether in early 1970. Leyland Australia believed that it would be perceived as an

Australian car rather than a British one, and that this would reap useful benefits in the marketplace. Their aim was to achieve monthly sales of 1500 cars, as against the average of 1,000 a month that the 1800 had achieved.

Even though the new stop-gap YDO13 was to be based heavily on the ADO17, it had to be made to look different. To that end, Roy Haynes, then BMC chief stylist in the UK, was

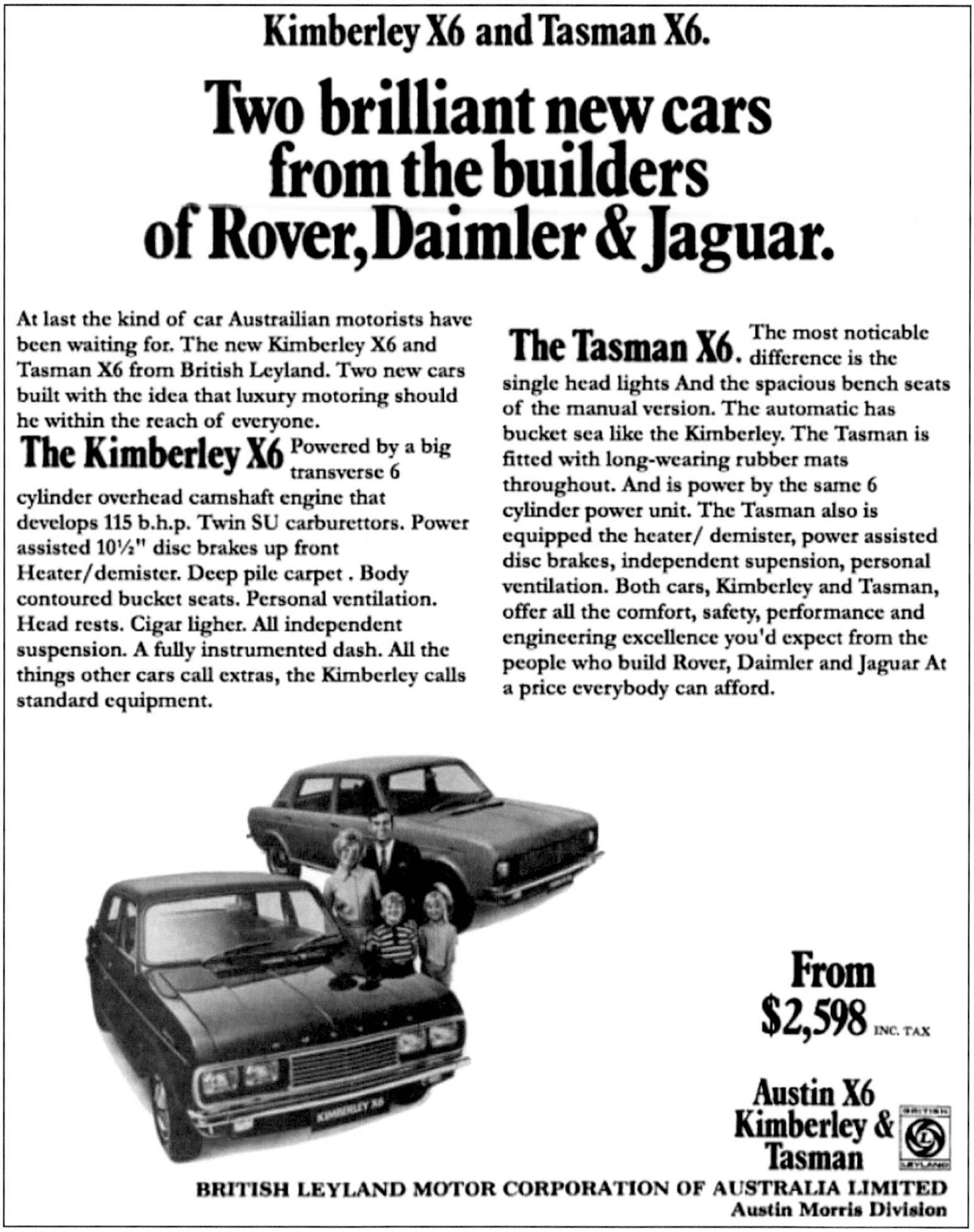

BLMC in Australia pushed the new six-cylinder Tasman and Kimberley models as hard as they could, by stressing the link with Rover, Daimler, and Jaguar products.

Meanwhile, the New Zealand Motor Corporation promoted the six-cylinder models like this. It was a pity that the ad copywriter could not spell 'Kimberley'...

given the job. He successfully made the car look distinctive by grafting on new front and rear ends. The rear gained a larger boot and the front was given a new full-width grille that tended to make the car look even wider than it already was. Both factors were important to make YDO13 competitive in the six-cylinder class in Australia and to foster the perception that it was a bigger car than the four-cylinder ADO17 it was replacing.

Other dimensions were reshuffled during development, and the new Australian car gained an extra 2 inches in the wheelbase. Its bodyshell was always intended for Australian manufacture, of course, and shared its underframe, doors and roof panel with the existing ADO17 shell. The 1800's Hydrolastic suspension was to remain in the specification, and the Local Content programme for the car was to be much the same as that already in place for the 1800. A key difference, however, was that the new E-series six-cylinder engine was to be assembled in the Unit Factory at Victoria Park, using mainly locally manufactured components.

Above: The Tasman was the less expensive of the two X6 models, with single rather than twin headlamps. This example was pictured beside the Tasman Sea that inspired its name. (Firstplanetcar/Flickr)

Below: Testing, Australian style! Buyers were not expected to treat their cars like this, but Australian road conditions could be very harsh.

Above: The Kimberley was distinguished from the Tasman by styled wheel trims as well as its twin headlamps.

Below: The X6 dashboard was very much of its time, and though perhaps to Australian taste, it was barely an improvement on the ADO17 style! The steering wheel of course carries a Leyland symbol.

The plan was to market two different trim levels: a lower one to retain buyers who would earlier have bought an 1800, and an upper one aimed squarely at those who bought the leading domestic six-cylinder saloons, which at that time were Ford Fairmonts and Holden Premiers. Both models were to have a new one-piece plastic dashboard with Ford-style adjustable air vents at its extremities, but there were to be differences in the seating and the equipment levels. Both were also to have very Australian names, deliberately chosen to reinforce the 'Australian-ness' of the car. The entry-level car was to be called the X6 Tasman and the de luxe model would be the X6 Kimberley; in both cases the X6 tag was an important addition that reminded buyers these were six-cylinder models.

The Tasman was readily recognisable by its single-headlight front end, and it also had a single-carburettor version of the engine with a round 100bhp. The Kimberley featured paired headlights, and had a twin-carburettor engine with 115bhp. The Tasman had a bench front seat and rubber flooring as standard, while the Kimberley had bucket seats and carpets – not to mention reversing lights and both boot and underbonnet lights. Of course there were options as well, and the lower-priced Tasman could be ordered with 'super de luxe' wheel trims, reversing lights, bucket front seats and 165 x 14 radial tyres instead of the standard 6.95 x 14 type. For the Kimberley, the options were reclining bucket seats, radial tyres, and a fashionable vinyl-covered roof.

Not surprisingly, Leyland Australia also seriously looked into producing a new utility model with the six-cylinder engine. During 1971, two prototypes of the YDO14 model were constructed, mating a YDO10 bodyshell to a YDO12 Tasman front end and running gear. The Product Engineering division had completed all the documentation for the YDO14 and issued it before the programme was cancelled at the last minute. The reasons for the cancellation are not known but poor sales forecasts may have been unable to justify the expense of continuing.

One of the YDO14 prototypes was written off during crash testing. The second was pressed into service as a hack by the Experimental Department at Victoria Park and was later used by Engineering Services at the Moorebank plant in Sydney. It was sold into private hands but has since disappeared.

The Tasman and Kimberley models went on sale towards the end of November 1970, and sales of 1,062 cars in the first part month seemed promising. However, the honeymoon was soon over. During the twelve months of 1971, just 6,765 cars found buyers – an average of just over 563 a month even though there had been good months with sales around the 900 mark. This was worse than the 1800 had achieved, and nowhere near what Leyland Australia had been hoping for. Analyses of the reason for this failure do not all agree, but there is general consensus on a quality control problem. Another difficulty seems to have been that the car was perceived as smaller than its rivals from Chrysler, Ford, and Holden, even though interior space was more than competitive. Instead, Australians typically saw it as a rival for smaller cars like the Holden Torana and the medium-sized Japanese saloons – and against these, it appeared expensive.

Determined to keep sales alive until the planned new cars were ready, Leyland Australia initiated a programme to develop Mk II versions of the cars. These were known as YDO19 types, and that new designation suggests more differences from the Mk I models than there actually were. The bodyshell was unchanged, and the Kimberley was in fact downgraded

Above: The underbonnet layout of the X6 range is represented here by a Kimberley Mk II, which had the single-carburettor engine. (Jeremy, CCA 2.0)

Below: This is a Kimberley Mk II again. The interior was tastefully executed, if in the style of its times. (1961australian, CC by 3.0)

Above: This Mk II Kimberley, fitted with an optional vinyl roof covering in the fashion of its time, was brought across to Britain. (John Shepherd, CC by 2.0)

Below: This Mk I Kimberley is a Morris version, and carries the name proudly across the front of its bonnet. (Riley, CCA 2.0 Generic)

to share the single-carburettor engine with the cheaper Tasman. The revised models were introduced during 1971 and lasted for just over a year. Production ended in December 1972, and all cars unsold at that date were stamped with a build date of December 1972 on their compliance plates. There were many of them: just 4,367 cars had been sold that year, around 30 per cent less than in the previous year.

The programme to clear several thousand unsold cars led to a bumper January 1973, but there were still cars in the dealer chain when the keenly awaited new Leyland P76 was launched in June. With hindsight, it seems clear that the Mk II models had simply been unable to shake off the poor reputation that the first models had acquired. *Wheels* magazine reported on a Mk II Kimberley and concluded that, 'by average standards it's an excellent car'. It offered more interior space than its rivals, seat comfort was good and so was the quality of the interior trim. It was quiet, with good brakes, and both handling and roadholding were praiseworthy. Counting against it, though, were the styling of the dashboard and the cabin furnishings, the steering wheel angle (which was the same as it always had been in the 1800), the gearchange, and the performance – newly reduced by the change to a single-carburettor engine. There can be little doubt that a power-steering option would also have been a help to sales.

Trying to get the numbers up in these last years, Leyland Australia also shipped the Tasman and Kimberley in CKD form to New Zealand from March 1971. Assembly was at the New Zealand Motor Corporation's Petone plant near Wellington, and to satisfy New Zealand dealers both models were available with Morris badges as well as the Austin badges used in Australia. Unfortunately, the target buyers were not very enthusiastic. Exact totals are not available, but Mark Webster did quote sales figures for the month of August 1971 in his book *Assembly*. A total of 1,046 cars found buyers; there were 238 examples of the Austin Tasman, 324 of the Morris Tasman, 250 of the Austin Kimberley, and 234 of the Morris Kimberley – a fairly even spread which does not really allow any conclusions to be drawn.

AN IDEA THAT GOT AWAY

The Australian plan to develop two new models to cover the largest and most lucrative areas of the local market was shaped by a report produced in 1967. As an early suggestion for the larger 'Model B' car, a prototype was built in 1968 with a Rover V8 engine mounted north–south in the bodyshell of an Austin 1800 and driving the front wheels through a Borg Warner three-speed automatic gearbox and a complex transfer box.

Memories suggest that the engine had been modified to a 4.2-litre capacity with the aid of a flat-plane crankshaft. However, the idea of building such a car was short-lived, and from 1969 Leyland Australia decided to design and build its own large car, which became the Leyland P76.

The single prototype survived into the early 1970s but was subsequently dismantled and, according to rumour, its engine was shipped to the UK. Sadly, its eventual fate remains unknown.

TECHNICAL SPECIFICATIONS – TASMAN AND KIMBERLEY MODELS

Engine:
Six-cylinder OHC mounted transversely; front-mounted radiator
2227cc (76.2mm bore x 81.3mm stroke)

Tasman Mk I & Mk II, Kimberley Mk II	*Kimberley Mk I*
Single SU HS6 carburettor	Two SU HS6 carburettors
8.5:1 compression ratio	8.5:1 compression ratio
100bhp at 5500rpm	115bhp at 5500rpm
110lb ft at 2000rpm	119lb ft at 2000rpm

Transmission:
Four-speed manual with the same internal ratios as the 1800
Optional Borg Warner 35 automatic with the same internal ratios as the 1800
Final drive 4.187:1 (manual) or 3.833:1 (automatic); later changed to 3.862:1

Suspension:
Front suspension with upper and lower arms, locating tie-rods and Hydrolastic units
Rear suspension with trailing arms, Hydrolastic units and anti-roll bar
Front and rear suspension interconnected through Hydrolastic system

Steering and Brakes:
Rack-and-pinion steering
Front disc brakes and rear drums

Wheels and Tyres:
14in wheels with 6.95 x 14 tyres (185 x 14 radial tyres optional)

Dimensions and Weights:

Overall length	174.58in
Overall width	66.58in
Overall height	57.25in
Wheelbase	108.125in
Front track	56.3in
Rear track	55.5in
Weight	2513lb

Performance:

Maximum speed	93mph
0–60mph	16.3 sec
Fuel consumption	20mpg (Tasman)

6

ADO61 – The Austin 3-Litre

The Austin 3-litre was developed to replace BMC's big six-cylinder Farina saloons in the 3-litre class. Based on the ADO53 design, they came as the Austin A110, Wolseley 6/110, and Vanden Plas 3-litre; all would need to be replaced at the same time, and the logical plan was for a single model to be badge-engineered to do so.

In this case, that single model had a most unusual origin and had nothing whatsoever to do with Alec Issigonis, even though he was the BMC Chief Engineer and even though it would eventually use some of his favoured engineering solutions, such as Hydrolastic suspension. In fact, Issigonis supposedly wanted nothing whatsoever to do with the car that was developed with the project code of ADO61.

In the right colours, the 3-litre certainly had the looks for the class in which it was selling, as this 1970 model shows. (Graham Roberston, CCA 2.0 Generic)

A rear view of the same 1970 car makes clear that it has an automatic transmission.

ADO61 had its origins in some work that was done jointly with Rolls-Royce between 1962 and about 1964. Rolls-Royce were considering the need to produce a model that was both smaller and less expensive than their traditional cars, and they were also painfully aware that the future lay with monocoque designs and not with their traditional separate-chassis construction. This required new solutions, and collaboration with a company that was already dependent on monocoque designs made perfect sense. The chosen company was BMC.

Rolls-Royce were impressed with the spacious passenger cabin that had been drawn up for the new ADO17 model (which was not yet in production, of course). It was ideally sized to suit a smaller car, and a project that was known within the Crewe styling department as the Bentley Bengal was set up around it. The Bengal would be a traditional rear-wheel-drive car, with longer front and rear ends added to the ADO17 cabin section to give the overall proportions that Rolls-Royce customers expected.

The Bengal proposal was turned into a quarter-scale model in John Blatchley's styling department. Not surprisingly, the suggestion was also made that there might eventually be a second derivative with Rolls-Royce identification (and, apparently, an improved interior specification). So a second quarter-scale model was made, featuring Rolls-Royce front-end styling. It then became very apparent that the six-light glasshouse of the ADO17 passenger cabin was only too recognisable, despite the very different bonnet and boot sections, and as a result a third quarter-scale model was made, this time with what appears to be a pillarless glasshouse.

The Austin 3-litre started life as an idea for a Bentley that would use the centre section of the ADO17 bodyshell. The project was known as the Bentley Bengal.

This revised clay model for the Bentley Bengal was produced when it became clear that the six-window configuration of the ADO17 was all too recognisable.

The Bentley was not alone; this model was produced to explore how a Rolls-Royce derivative might look. The project code name in this case was Rolls-Royce Rangoon.

All this of course would have required additional engineering to prepare for production, and the cost and complication of that would have negated some of the advantages of using the ADO17 centre section in the first place. For this and other reasons, the Rolls-Royce project came to nothing – but BMC did retain two things from it. One was a proposal to put a new small Rolls-Royce six-cylinder engine into a modified version of the ADO53 bodyshell, and this famously reached production as the Vanden Plas Princess 4-litre R in 1964. The other was the idea of making a rear-wheel-drive car by adding new front and rear sections to the ADO17 centre section.

Development

BMC's George Harriman took this idea back to Longbridge with him, and put it forward as a way of developing the new 3-litre saloon model that the company needed. To cut a long story short, as Chairman and Managing Director he got his way, and in 1963 or 1964 work began on that very car – which became ADO61. Issigonis must have hated it, because it went against all his ideas of efficient packaging. Development was entrusted to a team under Ron Nicholls.

ADO61 took shape at Longbridge with those extended front and rear ends, and some stories suggest that Pininfarina contributed some ideas – although the final shape suggested

Dating from 1963 or 1964, this styling proposal was for a Riley derivative of ADO61. There was an MG proposal, too.

This publicity picture shows an early engine bay. There were some minor changes later, including to the position of the coil.

that, if they did, these were largely ignored. One point of particular interest is that the idea of badge-engineering entered the picture early on, and front-end mock-ups were created for both Riley and MG derivatives. They shared the twin-headlamp arrangement of the eventual production ADO61.

The new car's suspension was drawn up around the BMC Hydrolastic system, with the addition of a self-levelling system at the rear. Such a system had been suggested for the Bentley Bengal, but whether there were any stronger similarities is not clear. The Hydrolastic system had some differences from versions in other BMC models, though, and the rear rubber springs were mounted separately from the Hydrolastic displacer units. The self-levelling system was completely separate, with hydraulics powered by an engine-driven pump that maintained a pre-set ride height by hydraulic rams in the rear dampers. The combination of these two systems did deliver a car that rode supremely well, and that was exactly what BMC wanted for their new flagship model.

Traditionally, BMC's large cars had depended on an under-stressed engine of large capacity because this made a big contribution to the refinement that was expected of them. The existing C-series six-cylinder had been introduced with a 2.6-litre capacity in 1954 and then enlarged to 2.9 litres in 1959, but had limited potential for further development. Perhaps the major factor in BMC thinking was that it would need extra power for the car that would eventually replace the Austin Healey 3000, but the needs of ADO61 were also borne in mind when a programme to redevelop the engine was put together.

The programme was really a complete redesign that was based on the bore and stroke dimensions of the existing engine. Fundamental to the plan was the use of seven main bearings instead of the existing four, which would enable the engine to cope with higher power outputs and would also ensure the smooth running that the big saloon would need. This entailed a redesign of the cylinder block, and the engines team took the opportunity to make it shorter and lighter as well, reducing weight further by having ancillary housings cast from aluminium alloy. The cylinder head and manifolding were also redesigned to improve breathing and allow more power to be extracted, and by the time the design was signed off, what was still called the C-series engine shared very few components with its predecessor.

The ADO61 version of the engine was to be in a very mild state of tune, 118bhp being considered enough even though it was only a 7 per cent increase on the 110bhp of the old Farina models. In fact, there was clearly some confusion about the actual power output within the BMC publicity department, and although the press-release material claimed 118bhp, the Motor Show catalogue claimed 125bhp! To deal with this power and the accompanying quite healthy torque, BMC designers came up with a new four-speed all-synchromesh manual gearbox, and in the tradition of the earlier big six-cylinder saloons this was provided with the option of a Laycock overdrive for restful high-speed cruising. An automatic gearbox was an obvious option to specify, and the one chosen was the well-known Borg Warner Type 35 with three forward speeds.

The heart of any luxury car is its interior, and of course the Austin version of ADO61 had to be relatively straightforward in order to leave scope for more luxurious versions in more expensive and differently badged derivatives. So despite a traditional approach using wood and leather, the car was given a strip speedometer – modern, and perhaps even stylish, but not really in keeping with its pretensions.

However, the elephant in the room (almost quite literally) was that the large rear-wheel-drive transmission tunnel intruded into a passenger cabin that had originally

Traditional English luxury car touches are clear here: figured wood for the dashboard and on the door tops, and of course carpet on the floor. It was clearly easier to specify a bent gear lever than to arrange a remote linkage that would have located it more sensibly!

been designed for a front-wheel-drive car. While there was still more than enough room for comfort, when the car went on sale it would not take buyers long to recognise that this upmarket luxury saloon actually offered less space than the much cheaper 1800 models. A larger boot, though useful in itself, was no real compensation.

Prototypes of ADO61 were on the roads by the middle of the 1960s, and a good deal of testing was done on the Routes Nationales in France. BMC had clearly learned from their mistake with the 1800 models that had never been tested outside Britain until after they entered production!

Badge Engineering

As the basic design neared completion, BMC began to consider more variations on the base model, which appears always to have been thought of as an Austin. In addition to the MG and Riley derivatives considered earlier, the BMC studios now took a look at a Wolseley model, while Vanden Plas at Kingsbury were asked for their thoughts on a replacement for the existing Vanden Plas 3-litre.

The Vanden Plas design was presented in photographs as a mock-up, with the company's favoured 'DEV 1' number plate to make clear that it was a design under development. However, the car photographed was almost certainly real – and according to the Vanden Plas Owners' Club there definitely was an ADO61 prototype, which was later destroyed in a fire in one of the storage tunnels at BMC's Longbridge factory.

The Vanden Plas 3-litre design prototype showed how well the ADO61 front end would have worked with that brand's characteristic features. The chrome-framed elements on either side of the grille seem unfinished here; perhaps they were intended to become air intake grilles, or had been intended as alternative positions for the auxiliary lamps.

Vanden Plas tackled the problem caused by the familiarity of the ADO17 six-light configuration, although their solution was not wholly pleasing. The badging reads 'Vanden Plas Princess'.

Vanden Plas retained the main lines of the ADO61 saloon, but the Kingsbury designers did branch out on their own with a redesign at the rear of the glasshouse where the rearmost triangular side windows disappeared in favour of a wrap-around rear window. The front end, meanwhile, adapted quite well to the characteristic Vanden Plas grille, although the auxiliary driving lamps set into the lower section of the bumper were perhaps not a complete success. Identification was assured by hubcaps with the stylised P emblem at their centres and by rear badges that read 'Vanden Plas Princess'.

This mock-up was built in 1967, and it may be that BMC deliberately waited until the Vanden Plas proposals were in before they started work on the Wolseley design, which had to be less luxurious than the Vanden Plas but noticeably plusher than the standard Austin model. The design was built into a running prototype during 1967, apparently with an automatic gearbox, which brought no exterior visual surprises; as on the Vanden Plas proposal, the front end characteristics of the marque worked well on the ADO61 shape. The interior had the expected combination of wood and leather, and the dashboard had a fine array of four dials spread across burr walnut (or, at least, burr-walnut veneer).

It was probably this Wolseley prototype that was later fitted with a Rover V8 engine and used by Harry Webster, the former Triumph Chief Engineer whom British Leyland had moved across to run the Austin-Morris division. One of the ADO61's problems had been identified as lacklustre performance, and by December 1968, Rover had been prevailed upon to offer 200 3.5-litre V8 engines a week as a solution. Those who drove the Wolseley prototype remember it as handling better than any production ADO61, probably because of the light weight of the V8 engine.

However, by this stage the case for a Wolseley derivative of ADO61 was looking very weak. Sales of the base model Austin 3-litre had not yet achieved their expected levels, and BMC's merger with the Leyland group of companies in 1968 had put a very different complexion on the matter. A V8-engined Wolseley ADO61 would face internal competition from the acknowledged leaders of the British luxury car class, and would be nibbling at sales for the big Rovers and the new Jaguar XJ6 saloon. By force of circumstances, it had become unwelcome and so, good though it might have been, it was cancelled. The proposed Vanden Plas derivative was probably cancelled for much the same reasons.

The Wolseley front end worked well, too. This may be the car that was given a Rover V8 engine and earned high praise from those who drove it.

With the Wolseley name came more figured wood, and this cowled dashboard with its four round dials was a suitable improvement on the plainer design used for the Austin 3-litre.

The Wolseley would of course have had leather upholstery, and the door trims dispensed with the diamond-pattern top section of the Austin design.

In Production

Although a few pilot-production Austin 3-litre cars were built over the summer of 1967, volume production had not begun by the time the new model was announced to the press in the autumn, just before the Earls Court Motor Show at which it was to make its public debut. There had clearly been some hesitation about what to call the car at the last minute, and some early press pictures have captions that describe it as an Austin Westminster 3-litre. The link to the name associated with the Farina-styled cars that the car was to replace was nevertheless quickly dropped, and the car became a plain Austin 3-litre.

Even though the cars were to be built at the Cowley factory (traditionally the home of Morris), the press launch was held at Austin's traditional Longbridge home. In charge of the presentation was Raymond Baxter, who at the time was running Public Relations for British Motor Holdings (the company formed from BMC's merger with Jaguar). Witnesses remember him warming up his audience with a presentation about the new Austin, which was followed by the car itself being wheeled onto the stage. Polite applause was then followed by an embarrassing silence: the assembled journalists were distinctly unimpressed.

A single car was then displayed on the Austin stand at the Earls Court show, which opened on 18 October. It was priced at £1,470 11*s* 6*d* in overdrive from (inclusive of

The Westminster name was in the frame for a time, but the cars were eventually badged simply as Austin 3-litre. (Jeremy, CC by 2.0)

£275 11*s* 6*d* Purchase Tax) or £1,516 13*s* 4*d* with the automatic gearbox (inclusive of £284 3*s* 4*d* Purchase Tax). That positioned it comfortably below the latest Rover 3.5-litre, newly up-engined from being a 3-litre, at £1,999 3*s* 4*d*. Below it came the Wolseley 18/85 (£1,135 0*s* 3*d* in automatic form) and the Austin and Morris versions of the 1800 (£923 11*s* 11*d* in De Luxe form or £883 0*s* 8*d* in standard form).

The earliest Austin 3-litres were distinguished by front doors without quarter-lights, no side skirts, and a chrome finisher on each sill. Most noticeably, there were one-piece horizontal headlamps, even though all the early mock-ups had featured paired lamps and the body pressings had been engineered to accept them. Less visibly, the doors had traditional door handles and locking pins rather than the safety latches that would also be introduced later.

There were no customer sales just yet. Austin prepared a fleet of 100 cars that was distributed to a group of trusted customers who were asked to report their findings during an extended trial. Volume production actually began in the late spring and early summer of 1968, and proper customer deliveries with it. Early customer feedback was monitored and combined with press opinions and reports from the field trials fleet, and by Motor Show time in October 1968, Austin had decided on some revisions.

The new thinking was revealed in a change of name: from now on, the model would be called an Austin 3-litre De Luxe in all its forms. It came with more comfortable seats, improved sound insulation, better fittings, and some revisions to the dashboard, which

Above: This early publicity picture shows the ADO61 3-litre as it was announced in autumn 1967, with rectangular headlamps and other differences from the volume production cars.

Right: Another early car shows the first production style of front end

This early publicity picture shows that the six-window passenger compartment originally designed for the 1800 models was still immediately recognisable.

was still nevertheless rather plain for a car in the luxury class. The front doors took on quarter-lights, and the paired headlamps originally planned were reinstated. The Motor Show catalogue revealed that the compression ratio had been increased to 9:1, but the quoted power was now 123bhp; confusion clearly still reigned in the publicity department! There was taller final drive gearing, too.

The ex-factory prices remained as they had been a year earlier, but an increase in Purchase Tax in the meantime ensured that buyers would have to pay more. The automatic model now cost £1,576 18*s* 11*d*, of which £344 89*s* 11*d* was Purchase Tax. This was not at all unreasonable, when the big Rover had increased to £2,174 6*s* 1*d*, but many buyers must have looked closely at the increasingly popular 'executive' models from Rover and Triumph, which offered a lot less space but a lot more prestige and driving enjoyment for relatively little difference in cost.

Sales never really took off. The Austin 3-litre proved to be a case of the wrong car at the wrong time. Its chances had been torpedoed by the BMC (by then BMH) merger with Leyland, and it was also out of sympathy with its times. More compact, better handling 'executive' cars were making major inroads into the sales of the old 3-litre class, which had once been considered the preserve of company directors. The public became very aware of the car's relationship to the ADO17, probably thanks mainly to press reporting, and in later years it acquired the rather unflattering nickname of Land Lobster.

In itself, the 3-litre was by no means a bad car, but the British Leyland public relations team never seemed to make very much effort to promote it, and as a result it simply withered on the vine. The last examples were built in May 1971, and in around three years of proper production fewer than 10,000 cars had left the production lines. It was a sad fate for a car that had started out with a good deal of promise.

Only a year after the 3-litre's announcement at Earls Court, the cars had been revised to feature paired headlamps. This press advertisement was trying hard to present an up-market image.

If size counted for anything, the Austin 3-litre certainly had it. Unfortunately, the market was already leaning towards more compact luxury cars. (Vauxford, CC-SA 4.0)

The 3-litre was a highly unusual choice for police duties, but the South Wales Police used this one, which is seen escorting a railway engine on a transporter from the scrapyard at Barry to its new home in preservation.

TECHNICAL SPECIFICATIONS – AUSTIN 3-LITRE

Engine:
Six-cylinder OHV C-series, mounted north–south
2912cc (83.34mm bore x 88.9mm stroke)
Two SU HS6 carburettors
8.2:1 compression ratio; 9.0:1 from October 1968
124bhp at 4500rpm (figures varying between 118bhp and 124bhp were claimed)
161lb ft at 3000rpm

Transmission:
Four-speed manual with synchromesh on all forward gears; ratios 3.43:1, 2.17:1, 1.38:1, 1.00:1, Reverse 3.09:1; optional Laycock overdrive with 0.82:1 ratio
Optional Borg Warner 35 automatic
Final drive 3.91:1

Suspension:
Front suspension with upper and lower wishbones, and Hydrolastic units
Rear suspension with semi-trailing arms, Hydrolastic units, and self-levelling rear dampers
Front and rear suspension interconnected through Hydrolastic system

Steering and Brakes:
Rack-and-pinion steering with standard power assistance
Front disc brakes (10.4in) and rear drums (9in x 2.25in)

Wheels and Tyres:
14in wheels with 185 x 14 radial tyres

Dimensions and Weights:

Overall length	185.7in
Overall width	66.75in
Overall height	56.75in
Wheelbase	115.5in
Front track	56.25in
Rear track	56in
Weight	3290lb approx. (unladen)

Performance:

Maximum speed	100mph
0–60mph	15.7 sec
Fuel consumption	16mpg

7

Curios and Conversions

The ADO17 became the basis for at least two spin-off projects within BMC and British Leyland, and both this car and the ADO61 were the subjects of some fascinating aftermarket conversions over the years.

The ADO30 Coupé

Some elements of the ADO17 were borrowed for an abortive project to produce a high-performance coupé in the early 1960s. This was another car that might have been shared with Rolls-Royce (or, more specifically, their Bentley marque) if it had prospered.

The origins of ADO30 lie in a competition that was run in late 1961 by the Swiss car magazine *Automobile Year* to celebrate its tenth season in print. The challenge was to design a two-seater sports coupé that could be based on any one of a choice of chassis. It had to be genuinely practical, capable of being put into production within a couple of years, and not a pure concept such as American car makers favoured to showcase their talents. The winners were three German design students, and their prize was not only a sum of money but also to have the car turned into a running prototype by Pininfarina.

Their design was intended for an Austin Healey 3000 chassis, and Pininfarina secured an appropriate chassis for its part in the programme, making only minor alterations to the original design. The resulting car was displayed on the Pininfarina stand at the 1962 Earls Court Show alongside a Ferrari Superamerica, at the Turin Show later that year, and then again at the Geneva Show in 1963.

Unsurprisingly, it attracted the attention of BMC's George Harriman, who acquired the rights to the coupé design for his company. His ambitious idea was to make the car into a competitor for the recently introduced Jaguar E-type. BMC gave the code of ADO30 to the project to turn it into a production model, while Issigonis knew it as engineering project XC512.

At this time, BMC and Rolls-Royce were exploring the possibilities for future collaboration, and the BMC project therefore focused on a car with the 4.0-litre Rolls-Royce FB60 engine (which would later be used in the Vanden Plas 4-litre R). In due course, Rolls-Royce would

The prototype car built by Pininfarina became the basis for the ADO30 project that used 1800 underpinnings.

The basic design of the Pininfarina-built coupé was also used for this scale mock-up called the Bentley Alpha. The letters on the number plate are the initials of John Blatchley, the head of Rolls-Royce styling at the time.

develop a twin-cam conversion of this engine called the G60 that delivered up to 275bhp, making it a good match for the 265bhp of the E-type's 3.8-litre engine.

Harriman also wanted to use this car to make a technological statement on behalf of BMC, and to that end he determined to use Hydrolastic suspension. The platform under development for the ADO17 1800 models provided the hardware, and work went ahead on a prototype. Ron Nicholls ran the project, working to Issigonis. Unfortunately, the Hydolastic suspension did not prove well-suited to a high-performance sports car; racing driver Paul Frère tried the car for BMC and was unimpressed with its handling.

Rolls-Royce, meanwhile, had looked at building their own version of the design with Bentley badges, and their styling department made a scale model of what they called the Bentley Alpha. This was essentially the original design adapted to take a Bentley grille – which looked rather awkward on the low, sloping nose.

The Bentley Alpha went no further and, sadly, nor did ADO30. There were thoughts of using a more traditional suspension system (which would have removed all links with ADO17), ideas of a convertible derivative, and – after BMC and Jaguar had joined forces in 1966 – even of using Jaguar engines. None of these became reality, and the project did not survive the creation of British Leyland in 1968.

The SRV3 Safety Research Car

Crash safety was very much on the automotive agenda in the early 1970s, following an initiative by the US Department of Transportation to establish a development programme for what it called ESVs (Experimental Safety Vehicles). The idea was to hold a series of conferences, at intervals of nine to ten months, at which participating manufacturers would compare notes on progress, and the first conference was held in May 1971. However, the programme fell apart three years later, following major disagreements among the participating manufacturers. The DOT did promise to re-orientate the programme, but its best intentions became bogged down in bureaucracy.

British Leyland established its own safety research programme in this period, the first car being a modified MGB in 1972, which was known as SSV1, those initials standing for Safety Systems Vehicle. Two years later, it furthered this research through a series

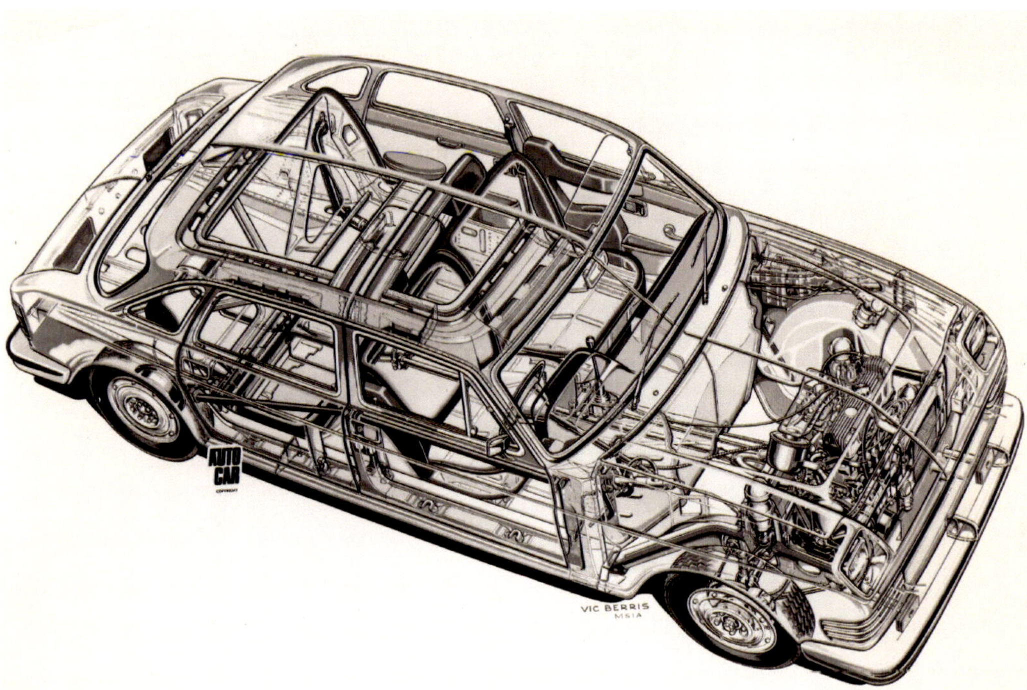

Vic Berris produced one of his superb cut-away drawings to illustrate the SRV3 for *Autocar* magazine, and BMC used it for a press release about the car dated 3 June 1974.

of five SRVs (Safety Research Vehicles) built in association with the Road Research Laboratory.

The first two were based on Morris Marinas, the fourth was based on a Mini and the fifth on a 1300. However, SRV3 was based on an ADO17, which was probably chosen to represent large saloon models. The earlier cars had all featured major front-end modifications associated with reducing the effects of front-end collisions, and SRV3 also had a modified 'shovel' nose with a large bumper designed to absorb impacts. An additional focus of the 1800-based car, however, was side impact protection, and to this end the doors engaged in dove-tail catches on the sills and featured reinforcing struts as well.

This was, of course, a pure engineering exercise, as the ADO17 was too near the end of its production life to take on any of these ideas. The SRV3 eventually disappeared from view, and was probably broken up.

Crayford

Crayford Auto Conversions was based at Westerham in Kent, and during the 1960s and 1970s acquired an enviable reputation for conversions of mainstream cars. The best-known examples are probably the convertibles based on various Ford models, but Crayford also turned their hand to several BMC models. Among them were the 1800 and the 3-litre.

The 1800 Hatchback

Beginning probably in October 1966, Crayford offered what they called an estate conversion of the 1800, although to avoid confusion with their later 1800 estate conversion, this first one is described here as a hatchback.

Two different versions of the 1800 Estate were available. The less expensive one simply had a rear seat that could be folded forwards, so allowing longer loads to be carried in the boot and increasing the load area considerably. The more expensive one was a full hatchback conversion, with a custom-built tailgate hinged at roof height and supported on heavy-duty hydraulic struts. The folding rear seat was also included.

This Crayford publicity picture shows the company's hatchback conversion on a Morris 1800 Mk II. One of the air vents can be seen just behind the rear door handle.

From the outside, there was little to distinguish the full hatchback version from a standard 1800 saloon, although a close look at the rear of the body would obviously reveal the additional shut lines of the hatchback itself. Crayford also added air extractor panels in the rear wings, just behind the doors, and the converted car could also be fitted with a specially designed roof rack for additional carrying capacity.

This conversion was quite successful. Crayford's David McMullan remembered in his book *The Crayford Story* that his company built examples of the car over a period of twelve years, but the Crayford Convertible Club has suggested a more plausible figure of seven years. There is no definitive production figure, but the club claims that one dealer in the north of England sold eighteen examples alone. Sadly, survivors are almost non-existent today.

When first introduced, the folding-seat conversion was priced at £95 and the full tailgate conversion cost £180. David McMullan has added that the full conversion had increased to £214 by 1971. Even the introduction of the hatchback Austin Maxi in 1969 did not kill sales of the Crayford Estate conversion, although no doubt it deterred some potential buyers. The car was offered on all variants of the ADO17, including the Wolseley types, although the absence of records means it is impossible to say how many of each type were actually converted.

The 3-Litre Estate

It was in 1970 that Crayford followed up with a conventional extended-roof estate car based on the Austin 3-litre. This was a most imposing conversion, with long side windows behind the doors and a one-piece tailgate hinged at roof height. The extended roof panel was trimmed in vinyl, which probably helped to conceal where there were joins in the panelwork, and David McMullan remembered in his book that some of the roof work was done by the coachbuilder FLM Panelcraft in Fulham, with whom Crayford had a fraternal working arrangement.

The car simply looked enormously long, and Crayford promoted it as the only nine-seater estate on sale in the UK. Nobody was prepared to argue with that, although promotional

The Austin 3-litre served as the base for a massively capacious estate conversion by Crayford.

This advertisement for the Crayford estate makes the point that the conversion could carry as many as nine people – as long as at least four of them were children, of course.

Four in the back! The Crayford directors used members of their own families for publicity shots like this one showing a 3-litre estate.

By the time this 3-litre estate was pictured, it had clearly fallen on hard times, but the details of the Crayford conversion are clear enough. The tailgate was taken from an 1100.

material did note that there were 'both children's and adult's seats'. All the rear seats could nevertheless be removed to leave a cavernous loading area at the rear.

The conversion cost £595 on top of the price of an Austin 3-litre, which made this an expensive purchase. Short of a long-wheelbase Land Rover (which actually had ten seats), there was nevertheless nothing else quite like it on the market – and there was a big difference in comfort and refinement between an Austin 3-litre and a Land Rover. The Crayford Convertible Club has estimated that a total of eleven were built; David McMullan's recollection was that sales were 'tiny'.

The 1800 Estate

David McMullan remembered that Crayford built two conventional long-roof estate cars from the BMC 1800, and that they were delivered to the Road Research Laboratory (a branch of the Ministry of Transport) in November 1971. The Crayford Convertible Club suggests that delivery might have been later, as the inspiration for their design supposedly came from a May 1972 issue of *The Funeral Director* magazine, which had an advertisement for a Woodall Nicholson long-wheelbase funeral limousine conversion.

These cars were required as mobile filming units, and were to be used to record early crash tests as part of a road safety programme. The extended back body was needed to carry the filming equipment; the film crew would travel in the main passenger cabin; and the extended roof (trimmed in vinyl, again probably to cover a join) was surmounted by a flat platform that looked rather like a roof rack. This was intended to provide a stable working platform for filming. There was a hinged tailgate, and detachable ladders could be mounted to the rails around the filming platform to give access for the film crew.

At least one of these cars (registered EMU 196J in July 1971) was an Austin 1800S, finished in beige but with a contrasting dark colour for the vinyl roof covering. It has not survived, being last taxed at the end of 1984.

This special estate was converted from an Austin 1800 for the Road Research Laboratory.

The Wadham Ambulances

The interior space of the Austin 3-litre in tandem with its supremely unruffled ride made the car an obvious candidate for ambulance conversions. Leading ambulance specialist Wadham Stringer of Waterlooville in Hampshire already built large quantities of vehicles on BMC chassis (notably the LD van), and developed an ambulance conversion of the 3-litre.

The conversion was achieved by adding a new roof panel that increased the working height within the body and extended to the tail of the car, where wide-opening access doors were provided. A flat floor permitted carriage of a stretcher-borne patient, and these conversions were typically used for high-speed transfer work rather than as

This picture of a Wadham Stringer conversion shows clearly how the roof extension was shaped to fit the existing saloon outline.

This preserved Wadham Stringer ambulance belonged to the medical team at the Lockheed factory in the Midlands.

emergency-response vehicles; their task was to transport seriously ill patients from one specialist medical centre to another.

Records suggest that Wadham Stringer did thirteen of these conversions, and the London Ambulance Service is believed to have taken four onto its strength in 1970–72. Others were bought by factory ambulance services, and a small number still survive.

The Woodall Nicholson Hearses and Funeral Cars

Just as the interior space of the 3-litre gave the model an appeal to ambulance specialists, so it had an appeal for the builders of hearses. The company that took up the option was Woodall Nicholson, a long-established business based in Halifax, and its neat 'Norland' coach-built hearse conversion of the 3-litre not only sold well but was also awarded the Hearse of the Year accolade in 1970.

A less-expensive hearse conversion was also made available on the basis of the 1800, probably during the currency of the Mk II models and slightly later than the 3-litre hearse. Completing the set, Woodall Nicholson also developed an extended-wheelbase 3-litre for use as a funeral car. This was extended behind the rear door, making room for a longer rearmost side window and, as was usual, the extended roof was trimmed in vinyl. The conversion featured a middle row of folding jump seats to increase its passenger capacity to eight.

This advertisement appeared in *The Funeral Director* magazine for November 1970, promoting Woodall Nicholson's Norland conversion of the 3-litre.

Right: This Woodall Nicholson 1800 hearse once belonged to the BMIHT collection at the Gaydon Motor Museum.

Below: This extended-wheelbase mourners' car is also believed to have been a Woodall Nicholson conversion.

8

Motorsport

From quite early on, BMC seem to have recognised that the 1800 had the potential to become a winning rally car, and it made its rally debut in the 1965 Monte Carlo event. This first effort was 'deniable' in the sense that the cars were a pair of former press demonstrators that were entered in the name of the BMC Publicity Department rather than the Competitions Department. Neither DJB 94B (Raymond Joss and John Fitzpatrick, sponsored by ITN) nor AOB 987B (Tommy Wisdom, Courtenay Johns and John Sprinzel, sponsored by the *Daily Telegraph*) covered itself in glory, but both did at least finish the event, in 29th and 32nd place, respectively.

The 1800's next recorded rally outing ended much more successfully. A former development car, LRX 824E, was prepared for regular partners Brian Culcheth and Johnstone Syer to tackle the Alpine Rally in September 1967 and won its class. This encouraging result persuaded BLMC to enter a team of three cars for the January 1968 Monte Carlo Rally. KOC 391E was crewed by Brian Culcheth and Mike Wood, LOF 179F by John Sprinzel and John Ryan, and LOF 238F by Peter Jopp and Willy Cave. Culcheth's 24th place overall was enough to convince BLMC to prepare a new team of three cars for the Safari Rally in April, and after an extensive test programme that included work at the military Longcross grounds, ORX 661F, ORX 662F and KOC 391E were put into battle. Sadly, they did not do well.

Faced with these mixed results, BLMC still believed the 1800 might have a rally future, and in June Brian Culcheth tried again on the Acropolis Rally. His tenth place overall was not discouraging, and now LRX 824E was pressed into service again for Tony Fall and Mike Wood to drive in the Danube Rally in Romania in mid-July 1968, this time in Group 6 specification with a 136bhp twin-carburettor engine. To considerable surprise at what was by now BLMC, they won the event. Next came the Shell 4000 Rally in Canada, where Tony Fall and Denis Johnson finished seventh overall and second in their class in ORX 663F (which had started life as KOC 391E).

In practice, the 1800 never had a chance to take its potential much further, not least because of the closure of the BLMC Competitions Department. But it did make a name for itself in two rather special endurance events that took place at the end of the decade. The first was the 1968 London to Sydney Marathon, when a car driven by Paddy Hopkirk with

LRX 824E was the earliest 1800 acknowledged to be a 'works' rally car. It was pictured here on the Alpine Rally in September 1967.

Tony Nash and Alec Poole finished second overall, and the second was the 1970 London to Mexico World Cup Rally, where 1800s achieved three of the top twenty positions.

The London to Sydney Marathon, 1968

The London to Sydney Marathon was dreamed up in 1967 by Sir Max Aitken, the proprietor of the *Daily Express* newspaper, in tandem with two senior members of his editorial team. Influenced by the sense of despondency that followed the devaluation of the pound sterling earlier that year, they put together a plan for an event that the newspaper could sponsor and that would showcase British engineering to the benefit of exports.

The first Marathon was scheduled for November 1968, and the newspaper offered a £10,000 prize to the winning team. British Leyland, then only recently formed, saw it as a golden opportunity to gain some beneficial publicity, and chose the 1800 as the car most suited for the job.

A works team of six cars, plus one service car, was assembled. Five cars were prepared by the Competitions Department at Abingdon, and the other two by the Special Tuning Department. Three teams of drivers were selected, and the Army, Navy, and Air Force all fielded their own crews for the other three cars. Five of the cars were painted in the traditional BMC works colours of red with a white roof, though with anti-reflective matt black on the front panels. The sixth was painted white all over; this car was sponsored by the British School of Motoring and driven by the Royal Navy team. (As an aside, it has been suggested that the 1800's nickname of 'Landcrab' originated in a press report on this event that highlighted their red colour and their tendency to 'crab' sideways at speed on loose surfaces.)

Though outwardly fairly standard, the cars had some major differences from those available in the showrooms at the time. They were built up from bare shells, with aluminium skins for the doors, bonnet, and boot, and Perspex rather than glass in some of the windows. The boot floor and the suspension mountings were reinforced, and the suspension itself was based on that found on very early Mk I models, with anti-roll bars front and rear, while the rear end was fitted with the larger front Hydrolastic displacers to handle the extra load.

Engine capacity was increased to 1894cc, the cylinder head was re-worked by Downton Engineering, and an MGB camshaft was fitted. With twin carburettors like the latest 1800S (actually 1.75in SUs), this delivered 100bhp at the flywheel. There was a competition clutch, and the final drive had the 4.1:1 ratio of the early Mk I; the wheels, too, had the 13-inch size of the Mk I cars, although lightweight Minilites were used in preference to the standard steel discs. A quicker steering rack was also fitted.

As for the interior, it was fitted out for a three-man crew and the rear seat could be converted into a bed so that one crew member could rest while the other two drove and navigated. The driver depended on a large rev counter placed right in front of him, and several of the less important controls were relocated on the navigator's side of the dashboard. There was a Hydrolastic pump on the rear parcels shelf in case of difficulties, and the boot contained twin 13-gallon petrol tanks to give maximum range between fuel stops. That left no room for spare wheels, so two were carried on the roof.

Left: VLM 128G was one of the London to Sydney Marathon entries, and was driven by a Royal Navy team. It still survives. (Vauxford, CC SA 4.0)

Below: SMO 226G, finished in the traditional BMC Competitions red with a white roof, placed second in the London to Sydney Marathon, driven by Paddy Hopkirk. (Paul Brown/ Flickr)

Four of the British Leyland 'works' 1800s that entered the 1968 Marathon still survive. The Paddy Hopkirk second-place car, registered SMO 226G, belongs to the collection at the British Motor Museum in Gaydon. The Royal Navy car, registered VLM 128G, was acquired for preservation but was also subsequently used in anger. Its history includes use for many years by its BSM sponsors, who used it as a training vehicle for fast pursuit driving.

The London to Mexico World Cup Rally, 1970

The London to Mexico World Cup Rally was the longest and most ambitious rally of its kind when it was run in 1970. It covered 16,000 miles of road sections and special stages, interrupted by a sea passage from Lisbon to Rio de Janeiro. Nearly 100 cars set off on the rally from London's Wembley Stadium on 19 April, but only twenty-three of them reached the finish at Mexico City's Aztec Stadium.

The British Leyland works entries this time were Triumph saloons, Austin Maxis, and a lone Mini, but the success of the 1800s in the earlier London to Sydney rally inspired several privateer drivers to enter such cars in this event. The rally was won by Hannu Mikkola and Gunnar Palm in a 'works' Ford Escort 1850GT, but the 1800s put in an excellent showing. No fewer than three of them were among the top twenty finishers: in ninth place was car 54, crewed by Reg Redgrave, Phil Cooper, and Bob Freeborough; in 11th place was the one crewed by Ken Tubman, Welenski, and McAuley; and in 18th place was the ladies' team of Jean Denton, Pat Wright, and Liz Crellin with car number 91.

Some of the London to Mexico cars survive in preservation today, and can be seen at classic-car shows around the country.

'The Beauty Box' carried an all-female team in the 1970 London to Mexico event. NOB 284F has been restored and still survives. (myclassicuk.com)

Appendix

Production Figures for ADO17 and ADO61

ADO17

Austin 1800	Mk I	110,000 (approx.)
	Mk II	74,000 (approx.)
1800 & 2200	Mk III	37,000 (approx.)
		(Total 221,000)
Morris 1800	Mk I	36,000 (approx.)
	Mk II	46,000 (approx.)
1800 & 2200	Mk III	23,000 (approx.)
Wolseley 18/85		35,397
Wolseley Six		25,214
		(Total 105,000)

The figures for the six-cylinder Austin and Morris 2200 models are included in the Mk III totals shown above, and jointly account for 20,865 cars.

ADO61

Austin 3-litre	9,992